MW00988918

WHEN I SURVEY THE WONDROUS CROSS

REFLECTIONS ON THE ATONEMENT

Richard L. Floyd

Confessing Christ
Acton Congregational Church
Acton, Massachusetts

Copyright © 2000 by Confessing Christ

Published by

Pickwick Publications
215 Incline Way
San Jose, CA 95139-1526

All rights reserved. No part of this book may be reproduced, stored in a retrieval system, or transmitted, in any form or by any means, electronic, mechanical, photocopying, recording, or otherwise, without the written permission of the author.

Printed in the United States of America

Library of Congress Cataloging-in-Publication Data

Floyd, Richard L.
    When I Survey the Wondrous Cross: reflections on the
    Atonement / by Richard L. Floyd.
        p. cm.; sh20 02-29-00
    Includes bibliographical references (p.).
    ISBN 1-55635-037-6 (alk. paper)
        1. Atonement. 2. Jesus Christ--Crucifixion. I. Title

BT265.2.F57 2000
232'.3--dc21
                              00-027956

" . . . May I never boast of anything except the cross of our Lord Jesus Christ, by which the world has been crucified to me, and I to the world."

Galatians 6: 14

"When I survey the wondrous cross, on which the young Prince of glory died, my richest gain I count but loss, and pour contempt on all my pride."

Isaac Watts

CONTENTS

FOREWORD

Question: What did Jesus do? Answer: He taught us how to live right, to do good. So the catechism of 19th century modernism. P. T. Forsyth thought otherwise. Can we really live right and do good? Is Jesus only a Galilean moralist? What about "the cruciality of the cross"? Richard Floyd puts these same questions to a 21st century postmodernism. And does so with the help of Forsyth and some contemporaries of kindred spirit. In fact, he has worked up his own countercatechism in another new work, *A Course in Basic Christianity*, used profitably already by local congregations.

If we want to go beyond the Jesusology of a pop Protestantism or the sophisticated Jesus Seminar, then a high Christology of the incarnate Person and atoning Work must reclaim our attention. From it we learn that the imperatives of the Sermon on the Mount are not the simple moral counsels of "exemplarism" but radical commands that show us up for who we are—sinners in need of the divine mercy. How we get to be "at one" with the God with whom we are at odds is the historic doctrine of the "atonement." Pastor Floyd faced this issue early in his ministry. He saw a mainline church awash in the same moralism Forsyth targeted. Since then the author has returned ever and again to the "cruciality of the cross." We have here the fruits of that focus. The intellectual labors behind this work are themselves a remarkable thing, given the many pressures on a local pastor. But Rick has kept himself freshly attuned to the subject by overseas' sabbatical research, and has written from time to time about the atonement in journal articles.

The concluding chapter, a homily on the Abraham and Isaac story, demonstrates his ability to connect his research with the day-to-day life of parish ministry. His mating of serious doctrinal inquiry with the pastoral calling was recently recognized by his appointment as a pastor theologian in the Center of Theological Inquiry at Princeton.

The timeliness of this study has to do not only with its attention to solidities so desperately needed in today's preaching and teaching, but also with its relevance to the hour's ecumenism. The ground-breaking *Joint Declaration on the Doctrine of Justification* signed in 1999 by the Roman Catholic Church and the Lutheran World Federation takes up the objectivity of the atonement as well as the subjectivity of personal faith. *When I Survey the Wondrous Cross*, with its exploration of justification writ large in the atoning Work of Christ, could be a helpful resource for congregations and pastors gathered in local communities to study the *Joint Declaration*, especially so because Rick's long years of leadership in ecumenical affairs are reflected in his approach to this subject.

And what specifically is there in this work that makes it valuable for both pastoralia and ecumenics? For one, it puts the reader in touch with some of the important current literature on the meaning of the cross, whether it be the biblical studies of Martin Hengel, Gérard Rossé, Richard Bauckham and N. T. Wright or the investigation of the atonement by theologians Colin Gunton, Stephen Sykes, and Paul Fiddes. For another, it draws directly or indirectly on the giants of recent times that have struggled with the meaning of the cross, notably P. T. Forsyth and Karl Barth. But it is the fresh insights that come from the author's own encounter with these interlocutors that give special significance to this book. For all that, Dr. Floyd leaves it to the reader to do his or her own final weave of these richly colored threads. To encourage others to take up this invitation, here is one effort to sift and sort the many learnings to be garnered from this research and reflection.

P. T. Forsyth never lets us forget the centrality of the cross in its "substantive" rather than its reductively "illustrative" sense, Calvary as the very hinge of God's history with us. Here is the cruciform "scandal of particularity" that moves the world from alienation to reconciliation. Further, it is truly God with whom we have to do on the cross, suffering in human "mode of being" the judgment that sin deserves. This God of *holy* love does not indulge our perversities, yet is the very One who pays the penalty, the Judge judged. But real flesh and blood are on that tree for a divine-*human* Person does the Work of at-one-ment; the self-restraint of God gives Jesus the freedom to struggle with temptation and thus to render the perfect obedience required. And this objective deed of God in Christ cannot be what it is without the existential and moral consequences in our personal and public lives.

Is there another way to say these Forsythian things without the problems entailed in his sometime idiosyncratic formulations, ones noted in these chapters? Here's a try.

A reading of the Prodigal Son story through the lens of the cross takes up Forsyth's major themes. Jesus' tale of the father's welcome of the errant son is an anticipation of the Father's embrace of the sinner on Calvary. Neither the rigor of the earthly Semitic father nor the holiness of the heavenly Father can indulge the self-centered flight of the son/sinner. But the wrath over wasted substance does not descend on either prodigal. Where did it go? "There is a cross in the heart of God" said Charles Dinsmore. The broken heart of God is when the divine love absorbs the divine wrath (Luther) with its consequences, the suffering of God on the cross for the sins of the world. So too only the suffering love of the earthly father, mercy taking judgment into itself, can account for the rush forward to greet the returning prodigal. In both cases, the father and the Father "died a little death" that made possible the welcome home.

But in this understanding of the cross, why did the human Jesus have to die? To tell us of God's holy love that cannot be known by human lights? Yes, singular revelation is one purpose, but standing alone, it offers only an exemplarism in which Jesus shows something, but does not do something to change our relationship to the Father. To expose the depths to which sin descends by making perfection vulnerable to its assaults so the power of Powerlessness can achieve the victory, as in the famous fishhook and bait metaphor put forward by the patristic tradition? Yes, surely the full extent of our fall is shown by our murder of the human Jesus and vulnerability is victorious. Yet is the exposure of sin reason enough for Christ to die? What then of the standard satisfaction views that a sinless human was needed to take the punishment in our place? Yes, but how is there an equivalency of his punishment to that deserved by us, and where is the "crucified God" in this false juxtaposition of the angry Father and the gentle Jesus?

A case could be made that Calvin's three-fold office of Christ is able to honor the truths in each of these without their respective reductionisms. So the lasting contribution of this teaching of Reformed tradition as shown by R. S. Franks. The prophetic office honors the Galilean ministry touted by exemplarism, the priestly office affirms the sacrifice on Calvary on which satisfaction theories center, the royal office points to the Eastern Church's stress on the resurrection victory of vulnerability. And in all cases, the divine-human Person does the atoning Work, the suffering and victorious God active in Christ's threefold ministry. But even this comprehensive scheme leaves questions unanswered. So we need a final caveat and last clue.

Therefore, a return to the prodigal son story. What triggered the father's response? The son's return, of course.

But the father's act was not evoked by a moral calculus—"he's back because he's sorry!"—for the father's run and reach began without knowledge of the return's rationale, while the son was "still far off." Forgiveness is not dependent on good works here, no more than on the cross; agape is unconditional.

In both cases some human event is inextricable from the release of suffering love toward the sinner: a prodigal son in the human story, an obedient Son in the divine story. There is no proclamation of how the compassionate God came among us without the account of Jesus on the cross, any more than there is a story of the father's embrace without the travel home of the prodigal. Finally, we are left with the narrative itself rather than a fully satisfying theory about it. And this is also where Pastor Floyd ends his inquiry, telling a story, significantly, a tale of another father and son, Abraham and Isaac. To love God "with all our mind" as we are urged by our Lord, we can and must explore the atonement seeking for a comprehensive view, wary of the tempting reductionisms. But it is not given to us to explain the atonement. And so Pastor Floyd's rightheaded and right-hearted final turn to Scripture itself and the stories great and small it has to tell. We can do no better than to follow him there along with the companions to whom he introduces us in his journey.

Gabriel Fackre

ACKNOWLEDGEMENTS

Atonement has been a theological preoccupation of mine for many years, and I have been privileged to have had two sabbaticals in which to study the subject. During the Trinity Term of 1989, I was a visiting scholar at Mansfield College, University of Oxford. I worked with Donald Norwood on the writings of P. T. Forsyth, with an emphasis on his soteriology and ecclesiology. A summary of that work appeared as "The Cross and the Church: Soteriology and Ecclesiology in P. T. Forsyth," *The Andover Newton Theological Review.*

During the Whitsunday Term of 1995, I was a Research Visitor at St. Mary's College at the University of St. Andrews. My research was on the Christian idea of substitutionary atonement, a continuation of the work I did at Oxford. I was privileged to have as my advisor Richard Bauckham, Professor of New Testament Studies, who was most generous with his time and attention and to whom I owe thanks for helping me get a much better grasp on this difficult subject. I want to thank Ronald A. Piper, Principal of St. Mary's College for all his assistance in the arrangements for my coming to St. Andrews and for his kindness during my stay. Most of these essays were first written at St. Andrews.

The essay on kenosis was written for a conference, "P. T. Forsyth: Theologian for the New Millennium" at the United Reformed Church Centre at Windermere, Cumbria, England, which took place in May, 1998, to coincide with the 150th anniversary of Forsyth's birth. My thanks to Alan P. F. Sell of the University of Wales at Aberystwyth for his kind invitation and to Alan Gaunt and Winifred Gaunt for their kind hospitality during our stay in Windermere.

The sermon, "The Lord will Provide" was preached at the Tabernacle at Craigville, Massachusetts on Cape Cod on June 27, 1999.

My thanks to those who made comments on the manuscript, especially Deborah Rahn Clemens, Gabriel Fackre, Alan P. F. Sell, and Charles Hambrick-Stowe. I am grateful to James Gorman who designed the cover. Lillian R. Carbin, the secretary at First Church, has been most helpful during the preparation of the manuscript. Lou R. Steigler provided valuable proof-reading. I am grateful to the Confessing Christ Movement in the United Church of Christ for a grant to help with publication and to Frederick Trost for his encouragement.

I must thank the people of First Church of Christ in Pittsfield, Congregational, for providing me with sabbaticals. Their ongoing commitment to a learned ministry should be a model for all congregations. Finally, thanks go to my wife Martha for all her support and to my children, Andrew and Rebecca, for packing up and following me on my adventures abroad.

Richard L. Floyd

INTRODUCTION

After twenty years in the ministry, I have become convinced that the cross of Jesus Christ needs to be at the center of both the church's life and its theology. My piety no doubt has helped to shape my theology, for it was the cross that led me back to the Christian faith as a young adult. Only Christian faith with a cross at its center was adequate to interpret for me the tragedies of my early adulthood, which at the personal level included the death of my mother when I was a teenager, and at the historical level included the assassinations of John and Robert Kennedy and Martin Luther King and the Vietnam War. While I was still in seminary, Moltmann's *The Crucified God* came out. I still remember a line from the Introduction, "What does it mean to recall the God who was crucified in a society whose official creed is optimism, and which is knee deep in blood?"

The "cruciality of the cross" (to borrow P. T. Forsyth's phrase), however, has by no means been self-evident in the churchly context in which I have lived during these past three decades. On the contrary, mainline Protestantism in America has tended to minimize the place of the cross in its preaching and teaching, seeing the cross as an offense to reason and morality. Jaroslav Pelikan's description of late nineteenth and early twentieth century theological liberalism still too often holds true: "The valid protest of the Ritschlian school against the mechanization of redemption by a vulgarized orthodoxy had all too quickly run out into a simplistic moralism. Therefore the reality of sin, the authority of the Law, and the power of the demonic were trivialized in liberal theology, and Jesus became at best a picture of God's love for mankind and at worst nothing more than one of the martyrs" (Preface to Aulen's *Christus Victor*).

More recently, some have seen the cross as an emblem of imperialism and anti-Semitism (see, for example, Mary Boys, "The Cross: Should a Symbol Betrayed be Reclaimed?" *Cross Currents*, Spring 1994) and, most significantly, a symbol of the abuse and victimization of women and children (Dolores Williams of Union Theological Seminary in New York is perhaps the best known American feminist holding these views). Williams suggests that we replace the cross with the more organic symbol of the mustard seed to raise awareness of the way societies "use and relate to nature and the religious effect of providing hope for human destiny."

These criticisms have some truth to them, reminding us that even Christians can be "enemies of the cross of Christ." Nevertheless, Williams's proposal is only the most blatant of a long tradition of theologians who would blunt or deny the cross. What many of these theologians share is a conviction that the cross is merely illustrative rather than constitutive for Christian salvation. If the cross merely illustrates the saving will of God, then it follows that it could just as well be illustrated by another symbol such as the mustard seed. Liberal Christianity since the Enlightenment has tended to view the cross this way, as merely a historical symbol of a timeless truth, and so is particularly vulnerable when that symbol comes under attack for a variety of perceived sins.

Over the years I have come more and more to view the cross as constitutive for salvation rather than illustrative of it. That is to say, that the coming of Christ, his life, death, and resurrection accomplished something rather than merely demonstrated something about God; accomplished something that we humans could not have accomplished by ourselves. So I am convinced that an adequate Christian soteriology will need to understand Christ's work in ways that re-appropriate pre-enlightenment views in a new way, reclaiming transcendence, and exploring concepts of "substitution."

Otherwise we will more and more lose a vocabulary that has, for generations, helped people understand the significance of the cross of Christ. The church today tends to understand the faith in psychological, political or managerial language and loses the powerful theological tradition that is the church's legacy. Many pastors are not much concerned about theology, and some consider historic Christianity to be the problem rather than the solution. The feminist critique has done us a backhanded favor by bringing to light the inadequacy of most of our thinking on the atonement. A church historian who teaches at one of our seminaries told me recently that as he interviews candidates for ministry he asks each one, "What does it mean to say that Jesus died on the cross for our sins?" He tells them that every graduate of the local fundamentalist Bible college will have a heartfelt and articulate answer to that question, and they should as well.

How one might best answer that question is my task here. I am convinced that the Bible's own vocabulary of atonement is still the best way to speak about the meaning of Christ's death on the cross "for us and for our salvation." Rather than putting forth a theory of atonement that stands apart from the biblical narrative, I propose that we regard the cross as the climax of the story of God. Which is to say that the crucifixion of Jesus can best be understood in the light of the whole story of Israel's God as told in the narrative of the Old Testament and in the words, deeds, and dramatic actions of Jesus prior to Good Friday (see, for example, N. T. Wright's *Jesus and the Victory of God*). It seems clear to me that the earliest Christians were able to interpret the death of Jesus as an atoning death because they could see how it was a part of the very same story of salvation that they had heard and known for so long. It was consistent with the identity of the God they knew (see Richard Bauckham's *God Crucified: Monotheism and Christology in the New Testament*), and they were able to recognize it in the stories and ideas they shared such as "the suffering servant" in Isaiah 53 and "the binding of Isaac" in Genesis 22.

The essays that follow attempt to address the important issues that must be addressed if we are to speak about the atonement in a manner that is faithful to the biblical narrative. Chapter One asks, "Is substitutionary atonement biblical?" Chapter Two rehearses the traditional problems associated with substitutionary atonement. Chapter Three looks at the soteriology of P. T. Forsyth, and Chapter Four examines in detail his kenotic theory. Chapter Five addresses the problem of appropriation as expressed through the writings of Paul Fiddes, a contemporary theologian. Chapter Six summarizes what we have learned from the other essays and lays out how we might now speak about atonement, and the concluding sermon gives an example of how the idea of atonement might be brought into the church's proclamation. It is my hope and prayer that these essays will encourage pastors and teachers of the church to return to this central aspect of our faith for the sake of our witness and ministry. For I am convinced of the truth of P. T. Forsyth's words when he said that "the church will be for the world just what it is made by its theology of the cross" (*The Church and Sacraments*, p. 13).

Richard L. Floyd

I

IS SUBSTITUTIONARY ATONEMENT BIBLICAL?

What I hope to do in the following essays is to re-examine the Christian idea of the atoning death of Jesus Christ on the cross and to address the question of whether we can still speak of that death as in some way a substitution, and if so, in what way? Can we do this in a way that is faithful to the shape of the biblical narrative, that avoids the moral and theological difficulties of earlier theories of penal substitution, and that speaks to both what God has accomplished for humankind and to the way Christians actually experience that salvation?

I want to begin by exploring the biblical origins of the doctrine of atonement with an eye out for ideas of substitution. Did the Christology of the early church include significant substitutionary elements? Can we sift out what the earliest interpretations of Jesus' death might have been? Will a theology of the atonement that speaks of substitution be congruent with the basic contours of the biblical narrative, and if so, what features of that narrative will inform such a theology?

Let me begin by looking at two recent studies which take a critical look at the cross and atonement of Christ in the Bible. They complement one another nicely as one is very deep, focused on one pericope of the Bible; and the other is quite wide, examining much of the biblical material and many extra-biblical sources. The first study is *The Cry of Jesus on the Cross: A Biblical and Theological Study* by Gérard Rossé, which is an extended essay on the significance of Jesus' death as told by Mark in Chapter 15:33-39. The second study is *The Atonement: the Origins of the Doctrine in the New Testament* by Martin Hengel, an English translation of an extended article with additions by the author.

Rossé's study argues that Mark's portrayal of the death of Jesus, in which the cry of abandonment from the cross is all that Jesus utters, expresses a pre-Markan theology that understood the abandonment of Jesus to be, in fact, not the denial of his messianic vocation, but the completion.

Rossé wants to rule out historicizing approaches to the death of Jesus, both those that attempt to harmonize the Gospel accounts and those that want to view the elements in the Markan narrative chronologically. Rossé instead insists that the Markan narrative needs to be understood as a theological interpretation of the death of Jesus and that the cry of abandonment is, in fact, the center of that interpretation:

> The value and importance of the cry of Jesus for Christian faith are in fact theological: the incarnate Son of God lives obedience and thus love for the Father to the point of completely assuming the human condition of suffering, of loneliness, of anguish, and of distance from God, of which the cross—as wood of the curse—is the sign. In the final analysis, the cry of abandonment must be understood as a revelatory word of God on the death of Christ. (p. 45)

In my view Rossé's thesis provides several important contributions toward a contemporary theology of the atonement. First, it reminds us of the theological nature of the narratives, so that our use of them can avoid the historicizing tendencies of so much interpretation in the past. Rossé doesn't believe that you can either prove or disprove the historicity of Jesus' cry by critically examining the text, but he does believe that the cry as it is narrated in Mark preserves a pre-Markan interpretation of the cross.

Secondly, Rossé's study reminds us to keep Israel in view as we try to understand the meaning of the cross. Here two motifs are particularly important: the suffering servant tradition and the fact of the cross being a curse according to the law. Referring to the pre-Markan tradition Rossé writes,

> By placing the destiny of the Messiah in the perspective of the *passio justi*, the young Church effected a theological upset of audacious originality: as the Just One, even the Messiah must undergo the destiny of the just of which the Scripture speaks; the Messiah himself must pass through suffering. This final consequence was not foreseen in the messianic expectation of Judaism and could not be explicitly understood from the Old Testament.

> The result is surprising: the Christian community was then able to see in the lamentable end of Jesus not the failure of his claim to be the Messiah but the confirmation that he really was so . . . .

> By this recourse to Scripture, by this understanding of the death of the Messiah, the Church succeeded in overcoming the principle obstacle, the scandal that Jesus and his death constituted for the Jews, and in giving this event its most profound interpretation. There is, in fact, in the event of the cross of Christ an aspect that distinguishes it from the just man persecuted because of his justice by the enemies of God. The enemies who mock the Crucified are the representatives of Israel. Jesus was condemned by observers of the law and in the name of the law.

> It is along these lines that the cry of abandonment acquires its full value in the pre-Markan

> tradition: this cry does not only express the con-
> sequence of the suffering endured on the cross
> as such; it is the rejection itself of Christ by Is-
> rael in the name of the law, experienced as the
> rejection of God. Jesus exits from the covenant
> of God with Israel. In Pauline terms, he has died
> through the law to the law (cf. Gal. 2:19); he
> has become a "curse" since "accursed is anyone
> who is hanged on a tree." (Gal. 3:13)

Rossé's attempt to recover a pre-Markan theological interpretation of the death of Jesus shows us, if his view is correct, that the early church interpreted the cross in ways that had both universal and eschatological implications. The cross was universal, in that Jesus in his abandonment took the place of every human being in the condition of alienation from God, estranged under the law:

> (Jesus) experienced death in all the tragic relig-
> ious meaning acquired as a consequence of sin:
> estrangement from God. He became, as Paul
> would say, "sin," a "curse" (2 Cor. 5:21; Gal.
> 3:13), and that to the extreme consequence of
> sin: death. The theological dimension of aban-
> donment now comes to light: *Jesus, the incar-
> nate Son, has completely assumed the human
> condition of estrangement from God.* (p. 67,
> italics mine)

The cross was also eschatological, in that this interpretation understands the abandonment not as a passive holding back by God, but as God's active intention. The cross was both "for us and for all men" and at the same time God's will. Unlike the death of a suffering martyr, which may inspire but cannot save, Christ's death is a divinely willed event, an eschatological event. So, even if the suffering servant provided some of the presuppositions for this interpretation of the death of Jesus it does not exhaust them. The pre-Markan tradition that Mark's narrative preserves insists on seeing both the universal and eschatological meaning of the event, and it may well be that Jesus' own actions and words at least in part provided some of the foundations for this interpretation. So Rossé can conclude:

> In this theological drama, manifested by the cry of Psalm 22:2, Jesus touches the depths of the trial of the suffering servant of Israel. But at the same time, he overcomes the Old Covenant and *attains the estranged condition of every man before God.* (italics mine)

> It is self-evident that the theological reflections by means of which the Primitive Church integrated the death of Jesus into its understanding of the faith do not at all contradict the possibility that it was the unfolding of the historical facts that drove the community to interpret the account of the crucifixion and death of Jesus in the light of Psalm 22—in other words, that the behavior of Jesus was at the origin of the theological reflection of the community.

> But once the theological imprint of the latter upon our account is admitted, one sees what consequences are contained in the affirmation that Jesus is the Messiah who has suffered the fate of the suffering servant and thus in the consideration that his death in the name of the law was willed by God.

Rossé shows how other features of the Markan narrative of Jesus' death highlight the eschatological and universal interpretation of the cross. The "darkness over the whole land" of Mark 15:33 is meant to show that the cross is an eschatological event, and the "torn veil of the temple" of Mark 15:38, in the same way, is meant to show the universal dimensions of the cross which overcome the old economy. The torn veil is now an opening into a new way for all humankind, overcoming the barriers that Israel constructed against the Gentile world.

> To see in the torn curtain—in relation to the death of Christ—both the end of the Jewish cult and the beginning of a new mode of God's presence is to see two meanings that are not mutual-

> ly exclusive . . . Jesus on the cross, totally emp-
> tied and opened, has become the new temple
> not made with human hands. The reality of the
> resurrection is tied, discreetly but certainly, to
> the image of the torn curtain as applied to the
> crucified Christ. (pp. 19-20)

Finally, Rossé suggests that this interpretation of the death of Jesus provides a way to understand the intratrinitarian life of God, not as some "closed circle in heaven" (Barth) but one that opens onto earth and involves it. In the death and raising of Jesus humanity "enters into this event between God and God" (p. 138).

In Martin Hengel's study he attempts to discover where the interpretation of Jesus' death as a vicarious atonement had its origin. Here is how he states the problem:

> No human death has influenced and shaped the
> world of late antiquity, and indeed the history of
> mankind as a whole down to the present day,
> more than that of the Galilean craftsman and
> itinerant preacher who was crucified before the
> gates of Jerusalem in A.D. 30 as a rebel and
> messianic pretender . . .
>
> The fact that this one Galilean was not forgotten
> but had a unique effect on world history, espe-
> cially by means of his death, is connected with
> the way in which this death was interpreted: it
> became the foundation of the Christian faith. In
> what follows, the most important question that
> we have to answer is: how did it come about
> that the disciples of Jesus could proclaim that
> cruel, disastrous execution of their master as the
> saving event par excellence? In other words,
> how did the crucifixion of Jesus come to take its
> place at the centre of early Christian preaching?
> How was it that this infamous death could so
> quickly be interpreted as a representative, aton-
> ing, sacrificial death, and in what interpretive

framework was such an understanding possible
at all? (p. 1)

Hengel wonders how the Gentile audience that
heard this strange new gospel of the crucified Messiah was
able to understand it. What categories prepared them for it?
Were such categories from the Old Testament or from the
Greco-Roman world?

To begin his inquiry, Hengel makes it clear that we
can no longer hold as tenable the oft-stated dichotomy between Old Testament and Jewish traditions and Hellenistic
traditions. This fruit of the "history of religions" movement
can no longer be held by those who wish to deal faithfully
with the facts of history. The Jews in the time of Jesus had
been living for four hundred years in a Hellenistic cultural
environment, even in the Palestinian mother country.

He then moves on to examine Greek and Roman
traditions to show that there were "a whole series of closer
and distant analogies" which can be found to "the interpretation of the death of Jesus as a presupposition of his exal-
tation and also as a representative atoning death for others"
(p. 4). Various examples of heroes securing their heroic
status by their death are provided. Strikingly, in contrast,
such glorification of martyrs is missing from the Old Testament traditions (p. 7).

Among the Greeks, on the other hand, there is a
strong developing tradition of vicarious deaths on behalf of
friends, relatives, and one's city-state. This tradition further
develops into sacrificial death for ideals, for truth or the
law, the best known example being the death of Socrates to
uphold the law of Athens even though he declared his inno-
cence from the charge against him (pp. 15-16).

Hengel writes that "In the early Greek period, the
sacrifice of an individual was also understood as an expiatory sacrifice to assuage the anger of the gods.... The theme

of expiation in the sense of 'purifying the land' from evil
and disaster or of assuaging the wrath of the gods was part
of the *lingua franca* of the religions of late antiquity" (p.
19). The Greek form of the scapegoat is a summary charac-
terization of these expiatory rites (p. 24).

He concludes that the pagan audiences in the cities
of the Mediterranean would have had no trouble understanding the new message of "the atoning death of Jesus
and the conceptions of vicariousness, atonement and reconciliation associated with it" (p. 28). It is rather people of today who have difficulty understanding these soteriological
categories. He warns against stripping away these dimensions for apologetic reasons: "Today we find not only 'fundamentalist' but also a radical critical biblicism, which
seeks to strip Jesus and the earliest Christian message, as
far as possible, of all that it regards as 'mythological' and
therefore as theologically obsolete" (p. 32). It is against this
approach that he calls for a critical search to understand the
interpretation of Jesus' death as an atonement in terms of its
earliest presuppositions.

So where did the soteriological interpretation of the
death of Jesus in the earliest church come from? To answer
that larger question, Hengel raises three other questions.
First, what specific feature distinguished it from the analo-
gous Greek and Jewish conceptions? Second, what is the
connection between this interpretation and the Old Testament and Jewish tradition, given that early Christianity was
a Jewish Palestinian movement? And finally, when did this
interpretation enter primitive Christianity? Did it arrive at a
relatively late stage as an interpretive element, or was it a
constitutive element of the Christian message from the outset? Hengel asks, ". . . is it inseparably bound up with the
Easter event itself? Indeed, in essence does it perhaps go
back to the words and actions of Jesus himself?" (p. 33).
He suggests that an answer to the third question will provide answers to the other two.

He begins this inquiry by examining Pauline formulas to determine, in so much as is possible, a pre-Pauline tradition about the meaning of the death of Jesus, since this brings us closest to the preaching of the earliest Christian community. He finds in Paul two stereotyped expressions about the atoning death of Jesus. The first, the so-called "surrender formula" has language about God "giving up" Jesus for our salvation, such as in Romans 8:32 where God appears as subject: "He who did not spare his own Son, but gave him up for us all" and in Romans 4:25 where there is a divine passive: "Who was given up for our trespasses and raised for our justification" (p. 35). These formulas may well have antecedents from the Old Testament, such as Isaiah 53 or perhaps Isaiah 43:3ff. The second expression, the so-called "dying formula," can be seen in Paul's summary of the Gospel in 1Cor.15:3b: "that Christ died for our sins according to the scriptures (RSV)" (p. 36). Paul elsewhere uses abbreviated versions of this formula.

Hengel argues that this second formula preserves the preaching of the earliest community. He writes, "Paul passed it on (1Cor. 15:3b) in fixed form to the young Christians in Corinth on the founding of their community, and he retains it unaltered five or six years later when he writes 1 Corinthians. The Christological basis of the Pauline kerygma has a firm shape and did not undergo any metamorphoses" (p. 38).

He goes on to examine the individual elements of the formula, both the subject "Christ" and the predicate "died." Around the middle of the thirties the messianic title "Christos" became a proper name in Antioch, although it no doubt kept its earlier messianic connotation for some time. The phrase "the messiah died" had unique significance:

> That the man Jesus died meant little, for many men were crucified in Jewish Palestine at that time; incomparably more astonishing was the confession that this man, Jesus, executed as a

> criminal, was raised by God. To say that the
> Messiah had died was a complete reversal of
> this. It was taken for granted that God would
> grant victory to the Messiah; the message of his
> death on the cross, however, was a scandal. For
> in the light of all our present knowledge, the
> suffering and dying Messiah was not yet a fa-
> miliar traditional figure in the Judaism of the
> first century A.D. (p. 40)

The starting point for the statement of the death of
the Messiah is found in the *titulus* on the cross on which he
died as depicted in Mark's passion narrative. Hengel wants
to warn that the various interpretations that make much of
the suffering servant go astray if they do not keep fixed that
it is the Messiah that is suffering and not just any man.
Mark's use of Psalm 22 (and elsewhere 69) are significant
largely because they are exclusively messianic psalms. For
Mark *"The Messiah alone is the righteous and sinless one
par excellence"* (p. 41).

But why did the Messiah have to suffer? Like Rossé, Hengel thinks Mark's narrative preserves an earlier tradition in which a universal and eschatological interpretation
of Jesus' death was decisive. And at the heart of that tradition was the idea that Jesus' death on a cross replaced the
atoning and saving significance of sacrifice in the temple,
replaced it with the revolutionary insight that Jesus' death
was, once and for all, a universal atonement for all guilt (p.
47).

This necessarily led to a break with the sacrificial
cult of the temple. Is the universal soteriological interpretation of the death of Jesus a secondary and later step forced
on the Hellenists compared with the primary experience of
the Risen Lord? Is Paul's witness characteristic of a unity
of Christian preaching on this matter? Did Jesus himself
provide some of the impetus for this interpretation? These
questions are indissolubly linked with the question of Jesus' own self-identity. In other words, did Jesus claim to be

the Messiah?

Hengel looks at the alternatives, and finds arguments that allege that Jesus was crucified only as a rabbi and a prophet untenable. "Easter . . . in no way explains how the alleged 'rabbi and prophet' became the Messiah and Son of Man—which also means the exalted Lord, *maran*, of the community—, in short, how 'the proclaimer became the proclaimed.' If Jesus had no messianic features at all, the origin of the Christian kerygma would remain completely inexplicable and mysterious" (p. 48). Hengel claims there is no comparable example in Judaism that could account for this claim:

> In the Judaism of the time there were some authoritative teachers and pious martyrs who were said to have been transported to heaven or taken into the garden of Eden after their deaths. Not one of them was made Son of Man or Messiah. Nor do we have any indication whatsoever that a martyr prophet could be exalted to be Son of Man through the resurrection of the dead. (p. 49)

Hengel concludes that the decisive statements were formulated in Greek before the conversion of Paul. Pre-conversion Saul was persecuting the Hellenists in Jerusalem for their offensive statement that "Christ died for us (our sins)."

> By means of the new kerygmatic formula of the saving significance of the death of the Messiah, the Hellenists stressed the radical newness of the once-for-all, eschatological atonement which had taken place on Golgotha, which had been made manifest by the resurrection of Jesus, and now had to be proclaimed by all men. Thus the formula represented a demarcation from the worship of the Temple, which expressed the fundamental, qualitative difference between the dying of Jesus on the cross on Golgotha and the ongoing sin-offerings on Mount

Zion. If one so desired, one might say that the
atonement achieved through Christ developed
its saving power directly, in the heavenly sanc-
tuary, and not just on the altar and in the earthly
Holy of Holies. In this way access to the direct
presence of God himself had been opened up
for the believer. (pp. 51-52)

For the sake of argument, Hengel raises possible objections from a historical and traditio-historical point of
view that this interpretation could have arisen in Aramaic
speaking Jewish Palestine at that time at all. First, that the
Temple cult still seemed to play a part for the Jewish Christians in Judea, but Hengel is convinced that the temple no
longer is a place for atoning sacrifice but rather a house of
prayer.

Second, could vicarious atonement have arisen out
of an interpretation of Isaiah 53, "the only Old Testament
text which could have prompted the beginning of this de-
velopment?" Hengel finds no conclusive evidence for this:

So far, we have no clear-cut text from pre-
Christian Judaism which speaks of the vicarious
suffering of the Messiah in connection with
Isaiah 53. Of course, this does not rule out the
possibility of such a tradition, and there are
some indications in favour of it, but the basis
provided by our sources is too restricted. At all
events, a suffering Messiah did not belong to
the widespread popular Messianic hope in the
time of Jesus and a crucified Messiah was a real
blasphemy. (p. 59)

Third, against those who minimize any contribution
from the Psalm, Hengel doesn't doubt that Isaiah 53 had a
shaping influence on the earliest kerygma. Neither the formula "the surrender of Jesus" nor that of his representative
"dying for many" would have come into being without the
background of "this mysterious prophecy" (p. 60).

Fourth, an argument is made for locating this interpretation of Jesus' death in Hellenistic Jewish Christian traditions since we seem to find pre-Christian references to the vicarious atoning effect of the death of a martyr only in Jewish Hellenistic texts, such as II Macc. 7:32ff., 37ff. and IV Macc. Hengel reminds us of his previous criticism of drawing too sharp a distinction between "Hellenistic" and "Palestinian Judaism."

Fifth, he looks at the "binding of Isaac" in Gen. 22 as an antecedent to the interpretation of atonement, but sees it more as a text on the future of Israel and its election.

Sixth, and finally, he looks at references to representative atonement in the rabbinic literature, referring the reader to the study by Lohse. He concludes that:

> . . . after careful consideration of all the sources indicated, we must agree with Jeremias and Lohse that the vicarious atoning effect of the death or even the suffering of a righteous man was not unknown in the Palestinian Judaism of the first century A.D., independently of the question of terminology. Objections against deriving the soteriological interpretation of the death of Jesus from the earliest Aramaic-speaking community are, therefore, at any rate unconvincing. There is nothing from a historical or traditio-historical point of view which stands in the way of our deriving from the earliest community and perhaps even Jesus himself. This does not rule out the possibility *that the earliest Christian message of the self-offering of the Messiah Jesus on the cross for the salvation of 'many' was an unprecedentedly new and bold—and at the same time offensive— statement* in the context of both Greek-speaking and Aramaic speaking Judaism, because of its scandalous content, its eschatological radicalism and its universal significance. (pp. 65-66 italics his)

Hengel is confident that the interpretation of the death of Jesus as an expiatory sacrifice for our sins originates from the "basic event which gave rise to the Christian community" (p 65). The appearances of the risen Christ gave the disciples, against all expectations, the assurance that God had recognized Jesus as the true Messiah of Israel. The earliest confession of the resurrection that "God has raised Jesus from the dead" was constructed on the basis of this experience. A new experience that transcended their everyday lives was now a reality. No wonder that they related the appearances of the Risen Christ with the expected eschatological outpourings of the Spirit. The church that took shape after Easter understood these events as the beginning of the end of the world and the dawn of the rule of God. They also understood the preaching and teaching of Jesus in new ways: "Jesus preaching about the coming of the Son of Man was now transformed in the light of the Easter experience into the kerygma of the Lord of the community, risen, exalted to the right hand of God, and still to come, and to some extent the rule of God and his anointed were already present in embryo form" (p. 66).

But another profound understanding of their human situation was wrapped up in the Jesus event, that of their own sinfulness and that of all humankind.

> . . . we should not overlook the humanly insuperable barrier which divided the disciples from their master. Between the kingdom of God breaking in with the resurrection and exaltation of the Messiah Jesus and the former disciples and followers of Jesus was the awareness of their utter failure and deep guilt. Again, it is Mark's passion which depicts everyone's guilt over God's anointed in an impressive way. This solidarity in sin unites all those involved here. No one is excepted, from Pilate and the soldiers in the execution squad, through the leaders of the people and the crowd which they goaded on, to the twelve, with Judas who betrayed Jesus and Peter who denied him, indeed to the women

> at the tomb who fled in utter confusion and in their fear failed to obey the command of the angel (Mark 16:8). Their flight is matched by the flight of the disciples in 14:50; thus they, too, share in the scandal which Jesus prophesied in Mark 14:27. In this way Mark brings the crucified Messiah face to face with the barriers of human guilt. Here we can really say with Paul in Romans 3:23, 'for all have sinned and come short of the glory of God.' (p. 67)

And this understanding may go a long way toward explaining the prior question of "why did the Messiah have to suffer?" Hengel shows how in the surrender formula quoted by Paul in Romans 4:25 the death of the Messiah and his resurrection from the dead are seen as an indissoluble unity: "Who was surrendered for our trespasses, and raised for our justification" (p. 70). Hengel says that "there is no clear way of pointing to a pure resurrection kerygma without a soteriological interpretation of the death of Jesus" (p. 70).

A final question remains: how did the disciples, on the basis of their encounter with the risen Jesus, come to understand the cross in this way? Hengel believes we are forced to look to Jesus himself, to his person and actions. He notes the interpretive sayings of Jesus in the Last Supper traditions in 1 Cor. 1 1:23 and Mark 14:25 as examples of the way Jesus showed the disciples how to understand his death properly. His words over the cup, referring to a ransom for many, put atonement within a universal interpretive framework.

So, despite the fact that from a formal point of view, there are various analogies between Graeco-Roman and Jewish conceptions of atonement and the interpretation of the early church, the representative universal atoning death of Jesus Christ is new, breaking through the conceptual framework of the ancient world.

The pre-Pauline community interpreted this death as an event which stemmed from God himself, and, therefore, at the same time "recognized the crucified one as the pre-existent Son of God and mediator at creation, whom the Father had sent into the world to redeem his creation (Rom. 8:3; Gal. 4:4; Phil. 2:6-11; 1 Cor. 8:6; Col. 1:15ff.)" (p. 74). Hengel concludes that we must therefore speak of the saving significance of the death of Jesus within a Trinitarian context.

In conclusion, both Hengel and Rossé argue that the death of Jesus was interpreted as a substitutionary and universal atonement by the earliest traditions of the Christian community and that these understandings may well have been significantly shaped by Jesus' own self-understanding of his death. The cross was an eschatological event, willed by God, and can be best understood theologically within the context of the Trinity. I posed the question at the outset: "Is substitutionary atonement biblical?" The answer must be yes! More than that, it was constitutive for the earliest Christian gospel and continues to be indispensable for any adequate Christian discourse on the meaning of the death and resurrection of Jesus.

II

PROBLEMS FACING THE IDEA
OF A SUBSTITUTIONARY ATONEMENT

Even if one accepts that the interpretation of
Christ's death as a substitutionary atonement is thoroughly
biblical, there remain any number of problems and objections to understanding it this way, especially if one is putting forth a view that claims for the cross both objective divine activity and universal implications for human
salvation. In addition, some of the particular theories of
substitutionary atonement that have been propounded in the
last several centuries have been cast in such bloodcurdling
terms as to discredit the idea itself. To understand the main
objections I turn to the following works, which lay out
some of the criticisms of substitutionary atonement theories: Vernon White, *Atonement and Incarnation: An Essay
in Universalism and Particularity*, (Cambridge: Cambridge
University Press, 1991); Gerald O'Collins, *The Calvary
Christ*, (London: SCM Press, 1977), especially Chapter VI,
"Atonement for All"; and Richard Bauckham, "Criticisms
of Penal Substitution," (unpublished paper, no date).

A theology that claims that universal reconciliation
came about through a historically particular event or person
faces many difficulties from outside as well as from within
the Christian faith. The "expanded view" of the universe in
the twentieth century makes the universal claims of the
Christ event incredible to many people. Widespread travel
and world-wide communications make religious pluralism
a fact of modern life and put a human face on the previous-

ly abstract "unsaved heathen" of former centuries. In addition, the conceptual difficulties of ideas like atonement and incarnation put pressure from within theology to abandon its traditional claims. The tendency in much recent theology is to solve these problems and objections by giving ground on both objectivity and universality. These theologies counter the outside pressures facing atonement by proposing that atonement is merely *illustrative of* rather than *constitutive for* salvation, and that salvation is particular and limited rather than universal in scope. White summarizes from Maurice Wiles *The Remaking of Christian Doctrine* to give a typical example of a theology that has responded to these pressures:

> (Wiles) proposes that there need be no more to the meaning of the passion of Christ than the following: first, a revelation of the character of God; secondly, an historical phenomenon effective in the transformation of people's lives. Thus he has no wish to deny that it concerns only the 'comparatively small proportion of mankind which has heard of and responded to the preaching of the cross'; to claim anything more would be 'chasing a will o'the whisp.' (p. 3)

White himself offers an atonement theory that attempts to preserve objectivity on God's part and the universal implications of God's act by using the language of *re-creation* rather than *retribution*. White wants to answer the modern objection to a theology that claims universal implications from a particular event. He phrases the question he wants to answer thus: "What is it about any particular act that could constitute possibilities for the effectiveness of every other act the agent undertakes in relation to other agents throughout time and space?" He rightly notes that such a form safeguards both the universality of divine action and the uniqueness of the particular event (p. 52). As White's title implies, it is an incarnational Christology that provides the locus for divine activity with universal human implications. To support his view he points to Paul's soteriology, expressed in terms such as 'one body,' in 'one spirit,' 'Christ's' and 'in Christ,' referring to E. P. Sanders recent work on participation in Pauline atonement theory (p. 58). White draws attention also to C. F. D. Moule's writings on corporate personality and to the Patristic idea of recapitulation as articulated by Irenaeus, where Christ is understood to be the representative of the whole human race (p. 59). White's soteriology here hangs on his Christology: "It requires that the man Jesus and the eternal God share a common personal identity, as subject of the same incarnational experiences."

He sees that "the life, death and resurrection of Jesus Christ constitute a particular experience for God which is then offered throughout all time and space with the potential to 'save' all peoples" (p. 87). The cross then, as here construed, is primarily an event in God's "life" and only secondarily an act in history. That lack of historical grounding shows elsewhere in White's essay, as for example, in the implications of his theory for personal faith and for the church, which seem strangely irrelevant. Since his position needs no human agency (such as the church) to witness to the Christ event, which seems to have accomplished all that is necessary in eternity, he avoids any charge of religious imperialism in the face of the world religions. To his credit he holds fast to the two elements that one wants in an atonement doctrine, objectivity and universalism, and tries to deal with the pressures facing atonement from the modern world.

But these more general pressures on theology from the corrosive effects of the "acids of modernity" are not the only objections faced by an atonement doctrine. There are objections from within theology as well. There are any number of ways to organize these. Gerald O'Collins, for example, summarizes these objections in three categories: (1) God misrepresented, (2) Christ misrepresented, and (3) mankind misrepresented. Let us look at each in turn:

(1) O'Collins wants to distance himself from atonement views in which God's character or nature is misrepresented. For example, some articulations of the atonement can too easily speak of God as a vindictive punisher. For O'Collins, Christ's death on the cross is better understood as retributive suffering freely undertaken for others rather than punishment imposed by God as a substitute for guilty humanity.

(2) Similarly, O'Collins thinks Christ is misrepresented by substitution language which inclines toward the impersonal and lacks the intentionality of the language of "representation." Representation implies conscious acceptance by free moral agents on both sides. He also wants to carefully limit the way we talk of sacrifice, avoiding talk of an expiatory sacrifice that propitiates the anger of God and wins forgiveness for humankind. He admits that Paul uses sacrificial language (as in 1 Cor. 5:7, 11:25; Romans 3:24f) but claims that Paul doesn't make much of it as either an expiatory sacrifice or as a sacrifice that brings a new covenant with God. The reason for this reluctance is because Paul sees God as the initiator of the Christ event.

> It was God who 'put forward' his Son to expiate human sins and usher in the 'new covenant.' Once we see the crucifixion as an act of God toward mankind, we can hardly turn round and speak of God sacrificing to himself. Likewise, any stress on Calvary's consequences 'for us' tends to exclude the theme if its consequences 'for God' and hence its sacrificial quality. Paul knows the cross to be an effect of God's saving will, not its cause. And that belief restrains the apostle's readiness to proclaim Good Friday as an atoning sacrifice which establishes a new relationship between God and Man. (p. 108)

Paul's understanding of Christ's role in the crucifixion includes both obedience to the Father and suffering undertaken for humankind. In two senses, then, he acted as our representative, becoming obedient unto death (Philippians 2:8) and dying for us (Galatians 3:13) (pp. 108-109).

(3) Finally, O'Collins wants to avoid articulations of the atonement in which mankind is misrepresented in regard to human involvement. He asks, "Does belief in atonement (i) fail to produce a sense of commitment and (ii) suggest a world that smells of masochism?" (p. 109). These are, in fact, opposite problems. In the first, believers in atonement reverently refer to amends made in the past by Christ and become complacent about the world around them. In the second case, a neurotic preoccupation with self-inflicted suffering is fostered. This latter is similar to the criticisms of the cross offered by some feminists, that it fosters a victim mentality among those already prone to victimization. While admitting that atonement theories can go wildly astray, O'Collins concludes that:

> . . . a healthy atonement theology invites well-founded action and acceptance. Just as the reconciliation and liberation brought by Christ impels believers to act in genuinely reconciling and liberating ways, so the atonement he made on our behalf should alert us to our responsibility for the good state of the moral order. (p. 109)

While O'Collins' caveat about the language of substitution is a good one in the light of the many impersonal and mechanical atonement theories that have been proposed, and his highlighting of the language of representation reminds us of important and often neglected dimensions of Christ's solidarity and identification with us and his freely-chosen way of obedience, I am not persuaded that we can dispense with substitution language altogether. Christ's death is a death for us and does for us what we cannot do for ourselves. That is substitution. Representation adds some important notes, but it cannot carry the whole melody.

Likewise, O'Collins' warnings about expiation are helpful in protecting against a notion that Jesus was sacrificed to the Father in some way, yet again I think expiation language is biblical and retains a place in any doctrine of atonement as long as we keep in view O'Collins' reminder that God is the initiator and not the vindictive punisher whose anger gets assuaged by the act. I wonder, too, about O'Collins' statement, "Paul knows the cross to be an effect of God's saving will and not its cause." On one hand, that is right, that the cross can be seen in retrospect to be entirely consistent with God's nature and character as seen throughout the biblical narrative to that point. On the other hand, to speak of the cross as an "effect" of God's saving will could be construed to support an illustrative soteriology rather than one in which the cross is understood as constitutive for salvation.

Richard Bauckham's paper outlines the four classical criticisms of the doctrine of penal substitutionary atonement as put forward by Socinus (Fausto Sozzini, 1539-1604), who was criticizing the logic of the Reformers. The four criticisms are (1) Satisfaction and forgiveness are incompatible, (2) Substitution is unjust, (3) Christ's sufferings are not equivalent to the punishment that sinners deserve, and (4) Substitution fosters antinomianism. Bauckham notes that Socinus makes his criticisms apart from the context of the Reformer's theologies and that he neglects two significant aspects of the Reformers' views of the atonement, (a) that the work of Christ is not the activity of a third party, but rather the divine Son of God become man, who has come into the world to do the Father's will for human salvation, and (b) that the purpose of the atonement was not merely to save sinners, but to reconcile them to God. He then discusses each criticism in reverse order.

(4) Substitution ought to lead to antinomianism. Bauckham notes that this charge ignores (b) above, that the atonement puts sinners into relationship with God, thereby

not leaving them unchanged. Such criticisms stem from a moralistic misunderstanding of Christianity. We do not first need to be good, we need first to be in a right relationship with God.

(3) Christ's sufferings are not equivalent to the punishment required. Bauckham concedes that this charge is unanswerable, that attempts to answer it have failed in the past, and that if anything like penal substitution is to be retained it must be shown that this quantifying of amounts of punishment is unnecessary.

(2) Substitution is unjust. Socinus says that substitution is doubly unjust in that the guilty party goes unpunished, and an innocent party is punished undeservedly. Socinus did not believe in the incarnation, but according to it, it is not that God spares sinners and inflicts their penalty on an innocent third party, but rather in Christ, God himself takes on the suffering instead of inflicting it on sinful humanity. This answers Socinus' charge about punishing the innocent, but leaves the charge that the guilty go unpunished.

Some sort of articulation of Christ's identification or solidarity with the sinner goes part way to meeting this objection and most atonement theories have elements of this in them, but by the standards of human law courts to which Socinus refers, these motifs of identification cannot be strong enough to fully overcome his criticism. Bauckham refers to Wolfhart Pannenburg's defense of this criticism where he charges Socinus with excessive ethical individualism. Bauckham goes on to illustrate this point by drawing an analogy from human courts of law. We can see in the criminal justice system, for example, how the punishment of an individual in some very real way punishes their family. In some cases this shared suffering, through active sympathy, might even be considered a kind of vicarious suffering of punishment that we could consider to not be unjust. This is outside the competence of the courts, of course, where 'each person must bear the penalty he deserves' is the proper ideal for administering justice.

> But in real life the interdependence of humanity is such that the innocent do as a matter of fact suffer for the crimes of others. Though sometimes we see this as evil and seek to prevent it as far as possible, in other cases we applaud it. The cases in which we applaud it are those of *voluntary fellow-suffering in love*. We recognise at this point that *love* goes beyond the ethical individualism in which the courts must largely deal, and that the vicarious suffering of love may and can go beyond the ethical individualism of the courts because it corresponds more fully to the reality of human life and relationships than the justice of the courts is able to do. (p. 8)

To speak of Christ bearing our punishment is only possible because God in Christ goes beyond the justice of human law courts.

Since Socinus' criticism stays within the analogy of human courts, those theories of atonement that have accepted that framework are most vulnerable to his criticism. But if God's justice in the cross transcends the justice of human law courts than the criticism is avoided. Bauckham says that he has hinted at how this happens by his description of what he has called "the voluntary fellow-suffering of love." "God's love in Christ enables him to accomplish what, as a judge in a human law court, he could not accomplish" (p. 10). To do this means going beyond the merely retributive understanding of justice which both Socinus and his opponents shared.

(1) Satisfaction and forgiveness are incompatible. Socinus uses the analogy of a debt, where if the debt is paid, the creditor is obliged to renounce any claim on the debtor. Neither mercy nor forgiveness comes into play.

Again, Socinus takes no account of the incarnation. Since it is not a third party but God himself who pays the debt, he balances the books, so to speak, by paying himself off, at a cost to himself. For Socinus, God is free to do as he wills in response to human sin—justice and mercy are seen as alternatives.

Penal substitutionary theory, however, makes two points against this view of God's freedom: (a) God is not free without cost to himself, and (b) The cost is necessary because God does not set aside justice when he exercises mercy; rather he forgives in such a way as to satisfy justice. Justice and mercy are not alternatives; and in the cross, God administers both without contradiction.

To sum up, the problems and objections to a substitutionary atonement theory come from both the outside world of modernity and from within the theological circle. The former seem either to be conceptual, such as how the particular can impact the universal, or socio-political, such as the "imperialism" of universal religious claims or the negative impact of such views on victims or on people's mental health. These outside pressures need to be addressed in formulating an adequate atonement theory, but, in my view, they are not decisive and must not be allowed to preempt the discussion. The modern theologies that have responded to these external pressures by giving ground on important features of traditional soteriology are uniformly unsatisfactory and in the end raise as many questions as they answer.

More challenging, I think, are the criticisms from within the theological circle. An attempt to make a credible case for an atonement theory that does justice to both the nuances of the biblical narrative and the experience of real people is difficult at best. Some of the pitfalls we have reviewed are as follows: views of God which are morally offensive, that see him as a vindictive punisher (or, on the other hand, failing to deal with sin and evil, which we did not mention); views which emphasize retributive justice at the expense of other elements, views which emphasize sacrifice so as to imply that Christ died to propitiate God's anger; views which separate God's justice from God's mercy; views that are moralistic or legalistic; views in which substitution language is used mechanically and impersonally, neglecting the intentionality of the cross and the dimensions of Christ's obedience; views which either emphasize the finished nature of atonement so strongly that they invite human moral complacency, or, conversely, views which develop a morbid preoccupation with self-inflicted suffering. To read this list is to quickly realize that there are partial truths imbedded within all these various misconceptions and distortions. The complexity of the biblical materials ensures that no one theory will be comprehensive. But awareness of the problems prepares us for the important task of asking which elements are profitable for a credible atonement theory and which should be avoided.

III

P. T. FORSYTH ON ATONEMENT

Now that we have examined the elements that are needed in an adequate theology of the atonement, having looked at the biblical basis for speaking about Christ's death as a substitution and some of the typical problems associated with that language, let us examine the theology of P. T. Forsyth (1848-1921) to see how it measures up to our several criteria. Does it have the necessary objectivity that one looks for in an atonement theology? Is Christ's death constitutive for salvation rather than primarily illustrative? Does he use the language of penal substitution, and if so, does he avoid the pitfalls we have noted that tend to arise from this language? Does he deal with the moral objections that accrue to substitutionary atonement, and does his theology avoid the mechanical characteristics of so many substitutionary theologies? Are Christ's humanity and solidarity with humankind safeguarded as well as Christ's divinity. Finally, does his theology adequately account for the human appropriation of salvation for the purpose of human sanctification?

For the purposes of this essay we will examine Forsyth's book *The Work of Christ* (1910) which is, along with *The Cruciality of the Cross* (1909) and *The Person and Place of Jesus Christ* (1909), the best expression of his mature soteriology, although soteriological concerns are present in all of Forsyth's mature writings on a variety of subjects. Forsyth tells the reader in the preface to *The Work of Christ* that it was a series of extempore lectures given in

July 1909 to a gathering of ministers and then later tran-
scribed from notes: "It will be seen from the conditions that
the book cannot pretend to be more than a higher kind of
popularization, though this is less true of the two last chapters, which have been more worked over. The style approaches in parts a conversational familiarity which would
have been out of place in addressing theological experts"
(p. xxx). As is typical of Forsyth's writings, the language is
dense and rhetorical and somewhat repetitive. Nevertheless,
The Work of Christ expresses an insightful and quite com-
pelling soteriology that grapples with both the biblical
sources of the doctrine and its history of interpretation.

The first question we want to bring to Forsyth's interpretation of the atonement is whether it is adequately objective, constitutive for salvation, rather than merely illustrative of salvation. For Forsyth, what is decisive about the
cross of Christ (by which he means the whole work of
Christ in life, death, and resurrection) is that it is an act of
God and not an object lesson. It is not what God in Christ
said or reveals that is decisive for salvation, but what God
in Christ did. The fulcrum on which this theology rests is
the notion of the holiness of God. God's love is not charac-
terized as affection, but as loving activity; if it is God's love
it must be holy love. The reconciliation that the cross of
Christ accomplishes is a divine act to meet the conditions
of holy love in the face of human sin.

Forsyth has a running polemic against those who
see the cross as the apotheosis of human sacrifice, a sacrifice then to be emulated by us. "If the cross is not simply a
manner of religion but the object of our religion and the site
of revelation, then it stands there above all to effect God's
holiness, and not to concentrate man's self-sacrifice" (*The
Work of Christ*, p. xxi). He contrasts the sacrifice of Christ
with all human sacrifice, using the true story of a Belgian
railroad signalman who saved two trains from colliding, un-
beknownst to the passengers, by throwing himself on the

tracks to hold a tie rod in place that could not otherwise be
moved because of a frozen switch. Forsyth compares this
with the death of Christ and tells in what ways they are the
same and in what ways they are different. Unlike the signalman's deed (he doesn't die, by the way), Christ's death
is not merely an example of human heroism. The signalman's deed inspires those who hear of his story; it resonates
with something in the human soul that only needs to be
brought out. But what Christ's death does is not to inspire
the natural sensibilities of the human heart and soul.
Christ's death accomplishes something objective that af-
fects the human heart and soul from outside rather than
bringing out some latent sensibility. "... there is a difference between Christ's death and every case of heroism.
Christ's was a death on behalf of people with whom the
power of responding had to be created" (*The Work of
Christ,* p. 15). What the cross accomplishes is not the eleva-
tion of the human soul, but a new creation effected by an
act of God who does not bring out the best in humankind,
but rather accomplishes reconciliation at the very point
where we are at our worst, in the face of human sin and
guilt and shame.

> What the work of Christ requires is the tribute
> not of our admiration or even gratitude, not of
> our impressions or our thrills, but of our selves
> and our shame. Now we are coming to the crux
> of the matter—the tribute of our shame. That
> death had to make new men of us. It had to turn
> us not from potential friends to actual but from
> enemies into friends. It had not merely to touch
> a spring of slumbering friendship. There was a
> new creation. The love of God—I quote Paul,
> who did understand something of these things—
> the love of God is not merely evoked within us,
> it is 'shed abroad in our hearts by the Holy Spir-
> it which is given to us.' That is a very different
> thing than simply having a reservoir of natural
> feeling tapped. The death of Christ had to do
> with our sin and not with our sluggishness. It
> had to deal with our active hostility, and not

> simply with the passive dullness of our hearts.
> (*The Work of Christ*, p. 19)

Clearly we see here an objective understanding of the atonement, albeit one with implications for human life and faith. Forsyth wants to safeguard the uniqueness of Christ's sacrifice against all attempts to see it as of a kind with human heroism, even those allowing it to be the pre-eminent example. If Christ's sacrifice shares any affinity with human heroism, it is not as exemplar but as foundation on which the others are made possible:

> If you took all the world, and made heroes of them all, and kept them heroic all their lives, instead of only in one act, still you would not get the value, the equivalent, of Christ's sacrifice. It is not the sum of all heroisms. It would be more true to say it is the source of all heroisms, the foundation of them all. It is the underground something that makes heroisms, not something that heroisms make up. When Christ did what He did, it was God doing it. That is the great, absolutely unique and glorious thing. It is God in Christ reconciling. It was not human nature offering its very best to God. It was God offering His very best to man. (*The Work of Christ*, p. 24)

The emphasis here is so much on the divine initiative, that the humanity of Christ fades somewhat into the background (one recent critic notes a hint of Docetism in some of Forsyth's works), but I think this is a result of polemic concerns against the overly humanized Christ of his day. Forsyth also risks Patripassianism by employing the phrase "God dying" (which may show his influences from Luther which anticipates Moltmann. Forsyth's noted "kenotic" Christology is articulated in *The Person and Place of Jesus Christ,* written the same year, and not here in *The Work of Christ*, but the influence of kenosis informs this work). Above all, Forsyth wants to be clear that the cross is God in Christ acting and not the sacrificial offering of a heroic man:

> The sacrifice of the Cross was not man in Christ pleasing God; it was God in Christ reconciling man, and in a certain sense, reconciling Himself. My point at this moment is that the Cross of Christ was Christ reconciling man. It was not heroic man dying for a beloved and honoured God; it was God in some form dying for man. God dying for man. I am not afraid of that phrase; I cannot do without it. God dying for man; and for such men—hostile, malignantly hostile men. (*The Work of Christ*, p. 25)

This stark contrast between God's holiness and human sinfulness in Forsyth's writings necessitates that the atonement does for us what we could not do for ourselves. There is, therefore, a substitution, but it is not punishment as it is often understood. The purpose of God's judgement is not retribution, but satisfying the conditions of holy love.

> Get rid of the idea that judgement is chiefly retribution, and directly infliction. Realise that it is, positively, the establishing and the securing of eternal righteousness and holiness. View punishment as an indirect and collateral necessity, like the surgical pains that make room for nature's curing power. You will then find nothing morally repulsive in the idea of judgement effected in and on Christ, any more than in the thought that the kingdom was set up in Him. (*The Work of Christ*, pp. 135-136)

Unlike those theories that see God's honor or righteousness as separate "attributes" of God and risk making them a "third thing" beyond God and Christ, Forsyth's moral construal insists that the judgement of God is merely God acting in holy love. Christ's free and obedient death, then, do in some way satisfy the requirements of God's judgement in holy love for the purpose of making humankind holy, but not as a punishment of Christ. Forsyth rejects the notion that Christ's sufferings are equivalent to the pun-

ishment that humankind deserves, saying that you cannot
quantify the holy love and judgement of God in such a way.
To the phrase "penal sacrifice," Forsyth wants to tread cau-
tiously and say both "yes" and "no," given the problems
those words have created over the centuries. The argument,
as you shall see, is difficult to summarize, so I quote it here
at length:

> Judgement is a far greater idea than sacrifice.
> For you see great sacrifices made for silly or
> mischievous causes, sacrifices which show no
> insight whatever into the moral order or the di-
> vine sanctity. Now this sacrifice of Christ, when
> you connect it with the idea of judgement, must
> in some form or other be described as a penal
> sacrifice. Round that word penal there rages a
> great deal of controversy. And I am using the
> word with some reserve, because there are
> forms of interpreting it which do the idea injus-
> tice. The sacrifice of Christ was a penal sacri-
> fice. In what sense is that so? We can begin by
> clearing the ground, by asking, 'In what sense is
> it not true that the sacrifice of Christ was pe-
> nal?' Well, it cannot be true in the sense that
> God punished Christ. That is an absolutely un-
> thinkable thing. How can God punish Him in
> whom He was always well pleased? The two
> things are a contradiction in terms. And it can-
> not be true in the sense that Christ was in our
> stead in such a way as to exclude and exempt
> us. The sacrifice of Christ, then, was penal not
> in the sense of God so punishing Christ that
> there is left us only religious enjoyment, but in
> this sense. There is a penalty and a curse for sin;
> and Christ, by the deep intimacy of His sympa-
> thy with men, entered deeply into the blight and
> judgement which was entailed by man's sin,
> and which must be entailed by man's sin if God
> is a holy and therefore a judging God. It is im-
> possible for us to say that God was angry with
> Christ; but still Christ entered the wrath of God,
> understanding that phrase as I endeavoured to
> explain it yesterday. He entered the penumbra
> of judgement, and from it He confessed in free
> action, He praised and justified by act, before

the world, and on the scale of all the world, the holiness of God. You can therefore say that although Christ was not punished by God, He bore God's penalty upon sin. That penalty was not lifted even when the Son of God passed through. Is there not a real distinction between the two statements? To say that Christ was punished by God who was always well pleased with Him is an outrageous thing. Calvin himself repudiates the idea. But we may say that Christ did, at the depth of that great act of self-identification with us when He became man, He did enter the sphere of sin's penalty and the horror of sin's curse, in order that, from the very midst and depth of it, His confession and praise of God's holiness might rise like a spring of fresh water at the bottom of the bitter sea, and sweeten all. He justified God in His judgement and wrath. He justified God in this thing. (*The Work of Christ*, pp. 146-148)

Can one make such a fine distinction between punishment and penalty? Sin's penalty seems like a natural consequence, whereas punishment needs personal volition from a personal agent, in this case, God. Forsyth wants to argue that Christ is not the recipient of God's anger. He is right in what he wants to avoid.

Another question that we need to put to Forsyth is the issue of human appropriation of salvation, and in what way is that accomplished. How does Christ stand in solidarity with humankind as a representative? Here Forsyth uses once again moral categories. It is the obedience of Christ that is decisive both as the effectual cause of his atoning act and its results for our salvation. For Forsyth it is the obedience of Christ that makes the cross the activity of the holy love of God. He would put the emphasis on sacrificial obedience rather than on obedient sacrifice. As a human act Christ's obedience was in moral solidarity with the whole human race; as a holy act it satisfied the conditions of God's holy love which is also his judgment. Forsyth uses the phrase "Christ's confession," by which he means the confession of holiness that only God can offer. Christ as human in moral solidarity with humanity makes this confession that only God can make, and in doing so shows his divinity. "If God's holiness was to be fully confessed, in act and deed, in life, and death, and love transcending both, it can only be done by Godhead itself" (p. 152). Christ stands as humanity's representative and not as a sacrificial victim propitiating an angry God. This becomes important for Forsyth when he turns to the effects of the atonement on human sanctification. Christ is able to accept judgement in our place because it is by a human act of obedience that he does so, an act which establishes in deed his solidarity with humankind, even a humankind that was itself incapable of such a deed.

> But would his acceptance of judgement for us be possible, would it stand to our good, would it be of value in God's sight for us, if He were not in moral solidarity with us? How could it? What God sought was nothing so pagan as a mere victim outside our conscience and over our heads. It was a Confessor, a Priest, one taken from among men. But then this moral solidarity is the very thing that also gives, and must give, Him His mighty and revolutionary power on us. What makes it possible for Him to be a Divine victim or a Divine priest for us also makes Him a new Creator in us. His offering of a holy obedience to God's judgement is therefore valuable to God for us just because of that moral solidarity with us which also makes Him such a moral power upon us and in us. His creative regenerative action on us is a part of that same moral solidarity which also makes His acceptance of judgement stand to our good, and His confession of God's holiness to be the ground of ours. The same stroke on the one Christ went upward to God's heart and downward to ours. (*The Work of Christ*, pp. 190-191)

We can see how Forsyth wants to make the connection between justification and sanctification by positing a

solidarity between Christ and humanity whereby our participation in Christ makes the moral power of his holiness
available to us in ways that are not available to us as natural
human beings. There is a heavily Pauline notion of participation "in Christ" behind all this, as well as a big dose of
eschatology as Christ presents to God proleptically a holy
humanity (or church, in other places) as the new creation
effected by his cross. For example:

> Not only, generally, is there an organic moral
> connection and a spiritual solidarity between
> Christ and us, but also, more particularly, there
> is such a moral effect on Humanity included in
> the work of Christ, who causes it, that that ante-
> dated action on us, judging, melting, changing
> us, is also part of His offering to God. He comes
> bringing His sheaves with Him. In presenting
> Himself He offers implicitly and proleptically
> the new Humanity His holy work creates. The
> judgement we brought on Him becomes our
> worst judgement when we arraign ourselves;
> and it makes it so impossible for us to forgive
> ourselves that we are driven to accept forgive-
> ness from the hands of the very love which our
> sins doomed to a curse. (*The Work of Christ*, p.
> 192)

There is something quite impressive about the way
Forsyth uses the Pauline categories to link sanctification
with justification so that the former does not appear as an
afterthought as in so much theology (and especially in
some of the Reformers). The Christian believer who is in
any way free of gross self-deception knows himself or herself unable to be consistently holy and righteous. Forsyth is
suggesting that in Christ, we are not only already justified,
as the Reformer so clearly stated, but we are also sanctified
by Christ's act through no help of our own. "Our sanctification is already presented in our justification. Our repentance is already acting in His confession. The effect of His
Cross is to draw us into a repentance which is a dying with
Him, and therefore a part of the offering in His death; and

then it raises us in newness of life to a fellowship of His
resurrection" (*The Work of Christ*, p. 194).

Forsyth's ecclesiology is therefore implicit in his soteriology. The church is the community that lives "in
Christ" as the already sanctified by the gracious act of
God's holy love in the cross of Christ, sharing in the new
life of reconciliation that God in Christ has given them. "To
die and rise with Christ does not belong to Christian ethic,
to the method of Jesus, but it has a far deeper and more religious meaning. It is to be taken into His secret life. It is a
mystic incorporation into Christ's death and resurrection as
the standing act of spiritual existence. We are baptized into
His death, and not merely into dying like Him. We do not
echo His resurrection, we share it" (*The Work of Christ*, pp.
194-195).

What about the traditional Socian charge of antinomianism that arises to greet the articulation of such a finished work? Forsyth would argue that there is no way to
sanctification but by deliverance from sin, and no one can
"un-sin" him or herself however he or she amends. If the
atoning thing in the cross is reconciliation and not suffering, then what Christ created in the atonement was a new
holiness in us and not a new suffering. What Christ offers
to God in the cross is the assurance (the old word is surety)
of humanity's holiness, which is a real holiness. In doing so
God is really swearing to Himself, or putting it better, "it is
the Creator's self-assurance of His own regenerative powers" (*The Work of Christ*, p 212). We now share His life.
Forsyth would say that it isn't Christ in you that is important, but you in Christ. That is where the believer has access to the power of the holy God. Our necessary repentance is made for us and empowers us to continue to repent
before the holy God, whose holiness we can only obey
through Christ.

The old theories of atonement stressed suffering too

much, and therefore couldn't show how the act of Christ that freed us from the guilt of sin could free us from the power of sin. Suffering in itself has no sanctifying power.

> . . . when excessive attention was given to the suffering of Christ, and the atoning value was supposed to reside there instead of in the holy obedience, the work of Christ lost in purifying and sanctifying effect, whatever it may have done in pacifying or converting. The atoning thing being the holy obedience to the Holy, the same holiness which satisfied God sanctifies us. That is the idea that the Reformers did not grasp, through their preoccupation with Christ's sufferings. But it is the only idea which unites justification and sanctification and both with redemption. (*The Work of Christ*, p. 222)

Finally, let us ask about the scope of the saving work of Christ in Forsyth's thought. Since it is Christ, the representative human, who effects salvation through an act of holy obedience in solidarity with all humankind, then the scope of salvation is universal, if not the appropriation. Forsyth asks hypothetically about the sanctity of a Unitarian who believes not in an atoning cross, or satisfaction for sin. Is his sanctity of no account before God? Far from it, he answers: "but from our point of view we must regard them as incomplete stages, which draw their value from a subliminal union with that completed and holy offering of Christ which He never ceases to see, however far beneath our conscious light" (p. 214).

To conclude, Forsyth's attempt to articulate a moral theory of the atonement satisfies many of the criteria we have looked for in an atonement theory. His understanding of the atonement is objective and constitutive. It uses the substitution language of the New Testament in a careful and creative way. It connects justification with sanctification and speaks of Christ's solidarity with humankind. The emphasis on the cross as deed keeps the theory from seeming to speak of things that take place in eternity as we have seen in some other theories. Forsyth has recently been accused of inadequately articulating a Trinitarian theology (Sykes, p. 14, in Hart) and that his emphasis on the cross leads him to neglect elements of the incarnation (MacKinnon, p. 109, Hart), and one can see the basis of the charges, but again I think one can also see both the Incarnation and the "Holy" Trinity at work in much of what he says, and the unsystematic format he employs opens him to such charges. His theology has an important contribution to make to any modern attempt at articulating an atonement theory.

IV

KENOSIS REVISITED

In the theology of P. T. Forsyth, the usual two-nature Christology of Chalcedon is replaced by a two-act Christology, with an act from the divine side and a corresponding one from the human side. The divine kenosis, or self-emptying, coincides with the plerosis, or self-fulfillment, of Christ. So if this is a kenotic theory it is a kenotic theory with a difference, for it is construed in moral rather than in metaphysical language. It is dramatic and active rather than static, in keeping with its object, the free God who acts in the man Jesus Christ.

The term kenosis is derived from the Greek *heuton ekenosen*, "he emptied himself." As a substantive it is used, in the technical sense, of the Christological theory which sets out "to show how the Second Person of the Trinity could so enter into human life as that there resulted the genuinely human experience which is described by the evangelists" (H. R. Macintosh, *New Bible Dictionary*; see also N. T. Wright, *The Climax of the Covenant*, for a comprehensive review of the history of the interpretation of Philippians 2).

In the late nineteenth century various Kenotic theories of the atonement had been popular among German Lutherans (i.e., Gottried Thomasius, W. F. Gess, F. H. R. von Frank) and with some British Anglicans, notably Charles Gore who gave the Bampton Lectures at Oxford in 1889. There are stronger and weaker kenotic views, but, in general, kenotic views of incarnation or atonement put forth the idea in one way or another that, in Christ, God relinquished some aspect of his divinity.

The kenotic approach was criticized for a number of reasons: that it was pantheistic, blurring the line between God and humanity; that it undermined the doctrine of divine immutability; that it jeopardized the Trinity, for a humanized Son empty of divine attributes could be no part of the Trinitarian life; that it failed to recognize the proper relationship between divine existence, divine attributes and divine essence when it claimed the former can be separated from the latter; and finally, that the kenotic Christ is neither God nor man and therefore doesn't solve the problem it sets out to solve. The popularity of the kenotic approach was already waning by Forsyth's day. This he knew, as well as the criticisms and difficulties. He wrote, "many difficulties arise readily in one's own mind. It is a choice of difficulties" (*Person and Place*, p. 294). So he takes pains in places to separate himself from some of the more vulnerable of the kenoticist's views.

Nevertheless, he does not shy away from the kenotic language as long as it is in his distinctive moral vocabulary. Although Forsyth's full treatment of kenosis will wait until 1909 with *The Person and Place of Jesus Christ,* we see a kenotic emphasis already by 1895 in a sermon on Philippians 2: 5-8 entitled *"The Divine Self-Emptying"* (later to appear in the anthology *God the Holy Father*). In that earlier treatment Forsyth already has in outline the two-act Christology which will be spelled out in the kenosis/plerosis scheme of *The Person and Place of Jesus Christ.* Where the critics of kenotic theories worry about loss of divinity Forsyth wants to view kenosis as constitutive of Christ's divinity. He understands Christ's self-emptying as the very act which makes him Lord. It is only because of his Godhead that Christ can empty himself and in so doing He fulfills his Godhead. So in this case limitation is understood as a power rather than a defect.

> Well, notice here that Christ's emptying of Himself is not regarded as the loss of His true Godhead, but the condition of it. Godhead is what we worship. Christ's emptying of Himself has placed him at the centre of human worship. Therefore He is of Godhead. We worship Him as the crucified—through the cross, not in spite of the cross. (*God the Holy Father*, p. 32)

One of the traditional objections to a kenotic theory is that if the divine nature is given up how can the subsequent human act be an act of God and therefore a saving act, since only God can save? But Forsyth's view of kenosis doesn't involve the loss of divinity so much as its self-retraction or self-reduction. This is language about a free personality who chooses to act and is known by his acts, rather than language about a deity known by his attributes.

From Kant, Forsyth acquired a metaphysical agnosticism; this keeps him away from using the language of two natures to understand how the human Jesus relates to his Godhead. Rather than thinking about Christ in the language of two natures, Forsyth wants more active categories. He refers at times to "two modes of being" and elsewhere to "two moral movements":

> Let us cease speaking of a nature as if it were an entity; of two natures as two independent entities; and let us think and speak of two modes of being, like quantitative and qualitative, or physical and moral. Instead of speaking of certain attributes as renounced may we not speak of a new mode of their being? The Son, by an act of love's omnipotence, set aside the style of God, and took the style of a servant, the mental manner of a man, and the mode of moral action that mark's human nature. (*Person and Place*, p. 307)

This "setting aside" is the language one would use

of a personal subject, and this is what Forsyth presses for, a move away from the terms of entities and their substance to the terms of personalities and their freely chosen moral acts. So:

> As the union of wills we have in Christ, therefore, the union of two moral movements or directions, and not merely their confluence, their mutual living involution and not simply their inert conjunction. Much that may seem obscure would vanish if we could but cease to think in terms of material substance or force, however fine, and learn to think in terms of personal subjects and their kind in union; if our minds gave up handling quantities in these high matters and took up kinds. It is the long and engrained habit of thinking in masses or entities that makes so unfamiliar and dark the higher habit of thinking in acts. (*Person and Place*, p. 346)

Forsyth believes that construing the act of God in Christ in dramatic and moral terms is truer to the witness of the New Testament than the metaphysical language of Greek Philosophy and the Fathers of the early centuries. It is also truer, he is convinced, to the Christian experience of an atoning saving Christ. There is a decidedly experiential dimension to Forsyth's understanding of Christian authority: "It is the evangelical experience of every saved soul that is the real foundation of Christological belief anywhere. For Christ was not the epiphany of an idea, nor the epitome of a race, nor the incarnation, the precipitate, of a metaphysic—whatever metaphysic he may imply" (*Person and Place*, p. 9).

Kenosis is then a moral necessity for the God who is holy love. The holiness of God requires the divine intervention of the atoning cross against human sin. For Forsyth God's holiness is his defining attribute, God's very nature. He writes:

> The holy law is not the creation of God but His

> nature, and it cannot be treated as less than inviolate and eternal, it cannot be denied or simply annulled unless He seems false to Himself. If a play on words be permitted is such a connection, the self-denial of Christ was there because God could not deny himself. (*The Atonement in Modern Religious Thought*, p. 79)

Again we can see how Forsyth's understanding of God in moral rather than in metaphysical terms leads him to the logic of the cross. Human sin requires a real atonement. For Forsyth the wrath of God is not some arbitrary anger, but the response of the holy God to the very antithesis of holiness, which is sin. Sin could be defined for Forsyth as the denial of holy love. So divine holiness reacts to human sin with wrath and judgement. Forsyth's theology takes sin and evil with utmost seriousness. God cannot tolerate sin. It threatens his very being.

> God is fundamentally affected by sin. He is stung and to the core. It does not simply try Him. It challenges His whole place in the moral world. It puts Him on His trial as God. It is, in its nature, an assault on His life. Its vital object is to unseat Him. It has no part whatever in His purpose. It hates and kills Him. (*Positive Preaching*, p. 366)

So God is not just love, but holy love at war with sin. Liberal theology knows only a benign mercy that overlooks sin without overcoming it. That is why it can do without an atoning cross. But a theology that takes God's holiness seriously must also take sin and evil seriously too and realize that they are at war. God must not only forgive sin, but destroy it by an atonement. During the First World War, Forsyth wrote these words to describe the holiness of God and the power of His holy cross:

> The great Word of the Gospel is not God is love. That is too stationary, too little energetic. It produces a religion unable to cope with cri-

ses. But the Word is this—Love is omnipotent
for ever because it is holy. That is the voice of
Christ—raised from the midst of time, and its
chaos, and its convulsions, yet coming from the
depths of eternity, where the Son dwells in the
bosom of the Father, the Son to whom all power
is given in heaven and on earth because He
overcame the world in a cross holier than love
itself, more tragic, more solemn, more dynamic
than all earth's wars. The key to history is the
historic Christ above history and in command of
it, and there is no other. (*The Justification of
God*, p. 227)

The phrase "the historic Christ above history"
points to Forsyth's high Christology. If Christ truly shares
in the Godhead, he cannot have been created or arrived in
time, but must have been God from before the beginning.
The idea of a pre-existent Christ is, of course, seen here and
there in the New Testament, most notably in John 1 and in
Colossians 1:15f. Forsyth's Christology requires such a pre-
existent Christ if the atoning cross is to truly be an act of
the God who in the beginning created the heavens and the
earth. Against the claim of "the history of religions school"
that such passages reflect Gnostic influences Forsyth wants
to argue that the earthly career of Christ requires that he has
been of the Godhead from before the beginning.

An important passage for Forsyth is Matthew 11:27:
"All things have been handed over to me by my Father; and
no one knows the Son except the Father, and no one knows
the Father except the Son and anyone to whom the Son
chooses to reveal him" (*Person and Place*, p. 81). He cited
this text against liberal critics to show that it was not just in
the Gospel of John but also in the synoptic Gospels that a
high Christology was present. He argues that pre-existence
is not some add-on to the Gospel, but an intrinsic feature of
the Christ who is God. The Gospel requires a pre-existent
Christ and Christian experience confirms it. For example he
suggests that Paul's affirmation of the pre-existence of
Christ came from his experience, that he "worked back

from the faith that all things were made for Christ to the conviction that, as the end was in the beginning, all things were made by Christ; and by a Christ as personal as the Christ who was their goal" (*Person and Place*, p. 269).

So Christ's kenosis is not just an act in time but an act that was established from beyond time: "Christ's earthly humiliation had to have its foundation laid in heaven, and to be viewed but as the working out of a renunciation before the world was" (*Person and Place*, p. 270). "His emergence on earth was at is were the swelling in of heaven. His sacrifice began before He came into the world, and his cross was that of a lamb slain before the world's foundation. There was a Calvary above which was the mother of it all" (*Person and Place*, p. 271).

What does the kenosis involve? What is given up? Forsyth speaks of the self-reduction of God's attributes rather than their destruction, they go from being actual to potential. It is not so much limitation as concentration. They are drawn in. He says that God's attributes, such as omniscience, are not destroyed but are reduced from the actual to the potential. "They are only concentrated. The self-reduction, or self-retraction, of God might be a better phrase than the self-emptying" (*Person and Place*, p. 308).

He gives a series of examples of how a personality might freely choose to limit himself: a wise vizier to a foolish young sultan who voluntarily takes a cup of poison meant for his master and dies a prolonged and debilitating death; a musical genius in Russia who knowingly chooses to dedicate himself to political associations that cause him to be deported to a life in Siberia where he can never play the violin again; a university student brilliant in philosophical pursuits who, upon the death of his father, gives up his career to take over the leadership of the family business (*Person and Place*, pp. 296-298). In each case a conscious choice, motivated by love, is made which limits the personality. In each case, something precious is lost, but more is gained, and love is the motivation of each choice.

In Christ's case the free obedient act of the cross is not just love, but holy love concentrated at one point. Forsyth argues that since holy love is the supreme category of the Almighty, and the object for which His omnipotence exists, how could His omnipotence be imperiled by its own supreme act? "The freedom that limits itself to create freedom is true omnipotence, as the love that can humble itself to save is truly almighty" (*Person and Place* p. 314). Far from imperiling the Godhead of Christ, the kenosis of incarnation culminating in the cross is the most powerful act of Godhead, even more powerful than the creation of the world.

> To appear and act as Redeemer, to be born, suffer, and die, was a mightier act of Godhead than lay in all creation, preservation, and blessing of the world. It was only in the exercise of a perfect divine fullness (and therefore power) that Christ could empty and humble himself to the servant he became. As the humiliation grew so grew the exaltation of the power and person that achieved it. It was an act of such might that it was bound to break through the servant form, and take at last for all men's worship the lordly name. (*Person and Place*, p. 315)

So it is fitting that "at the name of Jesus every knee should bend, in heaven and on earth, and under the earth, and every tongue confess the Jesus Christ is Lord, to the glory of God the Father" (Philippians 2:10,11 NRSV). Here in praise and confession are represented the whole of creation according to the cosmology of the day.

So kenosis leads to plerosis, self-emptying to self-fulfillment, and not just at the final vindication but as a process throughout the life of Christ. Kenosis by itself is inadequate Forsyth says:

> What we have chiefly in view is the sort of uniqueness in the man Jesus which is required for the final and personal gift of Godhead in him. Now for such a purpose a Christ merely kenotic is inadequate. . . . We have examined the kenotic, or self-emptying theories of such an act, and we have found them either more helpful or less. But whether we take a kenotic theory or not, we must have some doctrine of God's self-divestment, or His reduction to our human case. Yet, if we go no farther than that, it only carries us half-way, it only leads us to the spectacle of a humbled God, and not to the experience of a redeeming and royal God. For redemption we need something more positive. It is a defect in kenotic theories, however sound, that they turn only on one side of the experience of Christ, viz., his descent and humiliation. It is a defect because that renunciatory element is negative after all; and to dwell on it, as modern views of Christ do, is to end in a Christian ethic somewhat weak, and tending to ascetic and self-occupied pity. (*Person and Place*, pp. 328-329)

If kenosis by itself is inadequate what must be the corresponding plerosis? The question that Forsyth wants to address in his two-act Christology is how is the humanity of Jesus related to his Godhead? Forsyth wants to take seriously both the historic Christ and his Godhead. He turns aside the liberal view that Christ is the apex of the spiritual evolution that emerges into a divine height in humanity, the divine blossom of the race, or its "heaven-kissing hill" (*Person and Place*, p. 33). No, the historic Christ comes to save humanity and not to exhibit humanity's salvation. "The King makes the Kingdom, and not the Kingdom the King" (*Person and Place*, p. 334). It is an invasion not an evolution. "Man does not simply unfold to God but God descends and enters man" *(Person and Place*, p. 334).

It is not that divinity and humanity share in being, rather they meet in action. There are two movements, God to man and man to God.

> God and man meet in humanity, not as two enti-
> ties or natures which coexist, but as two move-
> ments in mutual interplay, mutual struggle and
> reciprocal communion. On the one hand we
> have an initiative, creative, productive action,
> clear and sure, on the part of the eternal and ab-
> solute God; on the other we have the seeking,
> receptive, appropriative action of groping, err-
> ing, growing man. God finds a man who did not
> find Him, man finds a God who did find Him.
> (*Person and Place*, p. 336)

> [The capital "h" on the last word is either a mis-
> print or, more likely, Forsyth's subtle way of
> saying that God finds man only in Christ.]

Thus Christ embodies these two movements in
which God and humanity meet. Forsyth says that in Christ
we have two things: we have the action of the Godhead
concentrated through one hypostasis (or mode of being)
within it, and we have the growing moral appropriation by
man's soul moving Godward of that action as its own. This
is the two-act Christology which is the heart of Forsyth's
project. It has God entering our world: "We have that divine Son, by whose agency the world of souls was made,
not now creating another soul, but himself becoming such a
soul" (*Person and Place*, p. 338). And he enters it to bring
man to God as Christ acts in his humanity to be obedient to
the will of the Father. Christ never ceases to be what he has
always been, but grows in consciousness of his divinity
through the unfolding moral crisis which he enters in the
world:

> . . . the history of Christ's growth is then a histo-
> ry, by gradual moral conquest, of the mode of
> being from which, by a tremendous moral act,
> he came. It is reconquest. He learned the taste
> of an acquired divinity who had eternally
> known it as a possession. He won by duty what
> was his own by right. (*Person and Place*, p.
> 308)

So Christ in his humanity shares the human reality

of growth. Human life does not begin as a finished article. "It begins with certain possibilities, with a destiny engrained in the protoplast; but it only passes from a destiny into a perfection through a career" (*Person and Place*, p. 345). So Christ grows by moral struggle. He is tempted, but without sin. Again and again he must freely choose the way to go. Throughout his life he grows in his consciousness of what he was, although not in Godhead itself, which he always had. Here Forsyth is able to speak of a progressive incarnation, although in very qualified language:

> We may speak of a progressive incarnation within his life, if we give it a kenotic basis. He grew in the grace in which he always was, and in the knowledge of it. As his personal history enlarged and ripened by every experience, and as he was always found equal to each moral crisis, the latent Godhead became more and more mighty as his life's interior, and asserted itself with the more power as the personality grew in depth and scope. Every step he victoriously took into the dark and hostile land was an ascending movement also of the Godhead which was its base. This ascent into Hell went on, from His temptation to His tomb, in gathering power. Alongside his growing humiliation to the conditions of evil moved his growing exaltation to holy power. Alongside the Kenosis and its negations there went a corresponding Plerosis, without which the Kenosis is a one-sided idea. (*Person and Place*. p. 349)

Kenosis and Plerosis together constitute two movements of a single act of God. The more Christ laid down his personal life the more he gained his divine soul. "He lives out a moral plerosis by the very completeness of his kenosis; and he achieves the plerosis in resurrection and ascension." (*Person and Place*, p. 300)

The moral struggle that Christ was involved in was the struggle to be obedient to the Father's will. It is the struggle to become a servant. What does Christ's becoming

a servant mean? It means that he took on a state of subjuga-
tion in which he was called upon to render obedience. What
Christ becomes by his kenosis is a servant, and it is the free
moral act involved in his obedience to the Father's will that
is decisive for his Lordship. It is not his suffering, but his
obedience, that makes him Lord. Forsyth rejects the idea
that what is satisfied in the atonement is God's wounded
honor or God's justice.

> We have further left behind that the satisfaction
> of Christ was made either to God's wounded
> honour or to His punitive justice. And we see
> with growing and united clearness that it was
> made by obedience rather than suffering. There
> is a vast difference between suffering as a con-
> dition of Atonement and suffering as the thing
> of positive worth in it, what gives it its value.
> (*The Atonement in Modern Religious Thought*,
> p. 67)

But although Christ takes on full humanity there is a
limit. He remains without sin, as he must for only the sinless one can accomplish the work of the Holy God against
sin. Forsyth counters the argument that this somehow
makes Christ less than human. He argues that Christ was
indeed tempted in every way that humans are, and that his
struggles were real. "Because Christ was true man he could
be truly tempted; because he was true God he could not truly sin; but he was not less true man for that" (*Person and
Place* p. 302). Forsyth suggests that kenosis involved the
limitation of Christ's knowledge of the impossibility of sinning. He put aside his omniscience, so that he didn't know.
But if he didn't know, it was because he chose not to know.
This makes sense of his human struggles as depicted in the
Gospels more than the docetic Christ whose exertions are a
charade. Clearly Christ's struggles must persuade us that he
took the possibility of sin seriously. In the Garden of Gethsemane, Christ agonizes over whether the cross is truly the
Father's will. Forsyth says that he chose not to know that
for him sinning was impossible, and in doing so, shared the

full human experience of temptation:

> . . . to his own experience the moral conflict
> was entirely real, because his self-emptying in-
> cluded an oblivion of that impossibility of sin.
> As consciousness arose he was unwittingly pro-
> tected from those deflections incident to inexpe-
> rience which would have damaged his moral
> judgement and development when maturity
> came. And this was only possible if he had, to
> begin with, a unique, central, and powerful rela-
> tion to the being of God apart from his own
> earthly decisions. So that his growth was
> growth in what he was, and not simply to what
> he might be. It was not acquiring what he had
> not, but appropriating and realising what he
> had. It was coming to his own unique self. I
> have already said that I am alive to the criticism
> to which such a position has been exposed, in
> that it seems to take him out of a real moral con-
> flict like our own. And the answer, you have
> noted, is three-fold. First, that our redeemer
> must save us by his difference from us, however
> the salvation get home by his parity with us. He
> saves because he is God and not man. Second,
> the reality of his conflict is secured by his ke-
> notic ignorance of his inability to sin. And third,
> his unique relationship to God was a relation to
> a free God and not to a mechanical or physical
> fate, or to an invincible bias to good. (*Person
> and Place*, p. 342)

For Forsyth the death of Christ is really a sacrifice,
but it is not to a sacrifice made to God as much as a sacrifice made by God. "Atonement to God must be made, and
it was only possible from God" (*Positive Preaching*, p.
365). Christ became sin for us, and took the penalty for that
sin on himself. So the cross is penal but God doesn't punish
Christ. The atonement is penal but it is not penitential. The
punishment of sin fell on Christ's personality, to his consciousness, but not to his conscience. There was no self-
accusation in it, since he remained sinless. Christ never felt
that God was punishing him. "It was the consequence of

sin, though not of His sin" (*The Atonement in Modern Religious Thought*, p. 85).

The cross is a sacrifice, Christ being both priest and victim. "The priest, in his grace, becomes the victim, and completes his confession of God's holiness by meeting its acting as judgement. To forgive sin he must bear sin" (*Positive Preaching*, p. 362). This makes for a priestly Christ, a priestly religion and a priestly church (see my *The Cross and the Church: The Soteriology and Ecclesiology of P. T. Forsyth*). Forsyth believed that:

> New Testament Christianity is a priestly relig-
> ion or it is nothing. It gathers around a priestly
> cross on earth and a Great High Priest Eternal in
> the heavens. It also means the equal priesthood
> of each believer. But it means much more. That
> by itself is ruinous individualism. It means the
> collective priesthood of the Church as one. The
> greatest function of the Church in full commun-
> ion with Him is priestly. It is to confess, to sac-
> rifice, to intercede for the whole human race in
> Him. *(Person and Place*, p. 12)

That is where the act of God in Christ becomes contemporary, in the priestly ministry of the whole church of Jesus Christ, where soteriology informs theology, and the kenotic Christ creates the servant church in each succeeding generation.

How would we assess Forsyth's kenosis/plerosis proposal? Its purpose is twofold: (1) to safeguard the full humanity of Christ against a docetic view, and (2) to assert against liberal theology the full participation of Christ in the Godhead. I think it succeeds on both counts. He depicts a fully human Christ as one engaged in a mighty moral struggle, freely acting finally in obedience to the Father's will at the expense of his own life. The human struggle is not passed over lightly, yet the whole action is seen as an act of God.

If "doctrine is the conceptual redefinition of the biblical narrative" (Frei) then has Forsyth done justice to the biblical narrative? Here, too, Forsyth has been successful for he has successfully kept Scripture clearly in view throughout. He deals with both the high Christology of John and the epistles and the human Jesus of the Synoptics, the one who went through the full experience of the passion. Donald MacKinnon wrote that "the realities of Gethsemane refuse to allow him (Forsyth) to neglect the extent to which the passion was suffused by a kind of terrible uncertainty" (Hart, *Justice the True and Only Mercy*, p. 108). Forsyth's captures that "terrible uncertainty" and the powerful moral drama that is the passion.

There is great rhetorical power to Forsyth's theology as he addresses issue after issue returning always to the cross as the center. In *The Person and Place of Jesus Christ* he offers a highly nuanced theological interpretation that tries to make sense of the meaning of the cross. His kenotic Christology attempts to explain the mystery of the incarnation and the inner workings of the atonement without using the metaphysical language of which he was so suspicious. Both Donald MacKinnon and Colin Gunton have criticized Forsyth for eschewing metaphysical language, particularly ontological language, and for his too easy dismissal of the truths of Chalcedon. I have to agree in part with Colin Gunton's charge that Forsyth imported a metaphysic through the back door; after all, when you talk about "modes of being" you are pretty close to metaphysics if not already there. Gunton is right when he says: "Forsyth's kenotic theory of the incarnation . . . is essentially an attempt to make logical sense of the incarnation conceived as something that really happened in human history. It thus belies his proclaimed lack of interest in metaphysical theories" (see Gunton's critique of Forsyth in *Yesterday and Today*, pp. 168-173).

Having acknowledged the charge, let me say that I

think Forsyth's attempt to articulate a Christology outside the usual metaphysical framework is part of what gives his writings such rhetorical punch and dramatic power. He is a good theologian, but he never stops being a preacher, which may account for his continued popularity with preachers. In some respects he anticipates the various canonical and narrative approaches that are associated with the "Yale theology" of Hans Frei, George Lindbeck, and their students. Like them (and like Karl Barth) Forsyth's theology is thoroughly exegetical and takes the final form of the canon as the decisive text. He doesn't eschew historical criticism, but recognizes that it is "a good servant but a dangerous master." Yet, unlike at least some interpretations of the Yale School, he insists that the Gospel is more than a cultural linguistic narrative which sets norms for a community, the church. For Forsyth it is also God's truth for the whole world. In this he remains decidedly evangelical, and his hermeneutic has an important experiential dimension. But this is not just any experience! Forsyth would have understood "experience" more along the lines of Jonathan Edwards' view of Christian experience than that of those today for whom autonomous personal or group experience is authoritative. He would have had little use for the idea of "re-imagining" God in light of our experience. "See to the Gospel," he said, "and experience will take care of itself." For Forsyth it is not human religiosity that matters. Rather, the primary actor in the drama of human redemption is always God in Christ, known chiefly by his great act on the cross.

V

HOW IS ATONEMENT APPROPRIATED?

A Contemporary View in *Past Event and Present Salvation: The Christian Understanding of Atonement* by Paul Fiddes

Fiddes' book, published in 1989, attempts to address the problem we have seen in all articulations of the atonement that stress the objective side: they often give the impression that some transaction takes place in eternity and leaves us wondering how that has anything to do with our life and our faith in the here and now. As Fiddes' title implies, he wishes to take seriously the present implications of the atonement as well as the reality of the past event. It is interesting that Fiddes' book was published at just the same time as Colin Gunton's book *The Actuality of the Atonement,* a study of speech about God that argues for a re-examination of views of atonement that take seriously a prior and redeeming act of God in Jesus Christ. Taken together these two books represent the state of theologies of atonement: Gunton would say that the exemplarist and illustrative views of the atonement inadequately describe the divine sovereignty and initiative in the Christ event, yet (Fiddes would reply) more objective views don't adequately make clear the connection between the past event and the reality of salvation for contemporary believers and all of humanity.

Although Fiddes must be considered formally to be a representative of the more subjective approach, he is a

highly nuanced one, and he rightly resists the caricatures
directed against this position, especially against Abelard,
who is the ritual straw man of the foes of the exemplarist
position. I first read this book in 1989, and found on re-
reading it many more indications that Fiddes doesn't neglect the divine initiative in atonement. It is rather the way
the divine activity is construed that sets him apart from
more objective views. For Fiddes God works very much in-
side the processes of nature and history. Punishment is
more the inevitable consequence of human sin than any divine settling of scores or satisfying of honor. Although he
uses substitution language he denies that Christ placates
God or satisfies some external requirement that is a necessity for God.

Throughout this study I have spoken of two sets of
opposites: objective/subjective and constitutive/illustrative,
often equating objective with constitutive and subjective
with illustrative. To some extent Fiddes defies this typolo-
gy. For Fiddes it is more a matter of emphasis than of pola-
rity. God takes the initiative in risking to suffer and change
and thereby does something for us that we could not have
done for ourselves, which sounds like the language of the
objective and constitutive views we have seen. However,
when Fiddes turns to regard how the atonement is appropriated by us now, he uses language more typical of the subjective and illustrative views we have seen. Two main influences seem to inform his view: (1) an appreciative re-
interpretation of Abelard's exemplarist view which empha-
sizes the power of suffering love, and (2) an openness to using the language of a suffering and changing God to speak
about the atonement. From these elements and others he
fashions an atonement theory that uses the language of loving relationships as the primary metaphor for atonement.
He argues that this language avoids some of the problems
inherited by the various prevailing metaphors for atonement, such as the metaphors from the law court, the battlefield and the temple. The language of relationships is very

accessible to contemporary people, where the traditional language is not (sacrifice, for example, is a dead metaphor, the Christian content now defines the idea rather than the other way around). Therefore, Fiddes view is attractive and has apologetic usefulness. It could also be argued that the language of loving relationship he uses is faithful to the biblical narrative. Such relational language for atonement is not as explicit as, say, Paul's use of juridical metaphors or as the writer of Hebrews use of sacrificial metaphors, but rather the language of suffering love lies behind and beneath all that God is to Israel, the church and humankind throughout the narrative of salvation.

Does Fiddes accomplish what he sets out to do, to show how the past event of the cross makes for present salvation? Or to put it another way, can we see in his view an idea of atonement that is not only about God's redeeming work in the past at one particular time, but also about God's continuing work of atonement, so that the appropriation of salvation is not merely an afterthought to a completed work?

To answer that question let us look at the shape of his argument. The book is divided into three parts, with Part I examining the issues, Part II looking at the various images, and Part III addressing experiences related to atonement. In Part I Fiddes begins by raising the problem of appropriation. He puts it quite succinctly:

> Theories of atonement do not always explicitly address the question of how a past event can affect our present existence; the issue underlies all the images, but it is often simply assumed that if something important happened in the relationship between God and his estranged world at one point in time, it is bound to affect it now. In this study it will be my aim to highlight the link between past event and the renewal of life in the present, both as we explore the traditional images of atonement and as we see how these relate

to some important areas of individual and social
experience. (p. 5)

He then goes on to outline the various historic
views of the human predicament, on the logic that the way
you pose the problem will affect the way you formulate the
answer. The prevailing metaphors for atonement mirror former views of sin understood as subjection to hostile powers
(victory), uncleanness (sacrifice), and disorder (penal satisfaction). Each historical period will find its own preoccupa-
tions calling for a different metaphoric emphasis. Therefore
modern views of atonement will need to address the frag-
menting of personality and the loss of social relationships
(p. 12).

Salvation is both event and process. He notes that
the hymns of popular piety invariably assert that Jesus
saves, but sermons on the atonement are more likely to imply that Jesus saved. To believe in a savior God is to believe that he is always saving. The restoring of relationships
is not a transaction, but a process, just as forgiveness is no
mere business but "a shattering experience." To link past
with present Fiddes argues for a view that affirms the unity
of creation and redemption. Creation involved God in cost
and pain from the very beginning.

God is always sustaining his creation and keeping it
from falling into nothing. In creation God gives freedom to
something over against himself; he limits himself by the
freedom of others, his creatures, and becomes vulnerable to
their decisions. In the very act of creation then, he must
preserve it from willfully drifting away into nothingness
and the void. From the act of creation onwards he faces the
tragedy of death, and seeks to win his own creatures into
free and joyous fellowship with himself (p. 22).

This idea of divine risk is important to Fiddes argument. He affirms the idea of the continual suffering of God,
that is, that the divine personality in all ages feels the pain

caused by human sin. Personal love always involves sympathy, used in its original sense of a "suffering with." So for God to love he must suffer with those whom he loves. We see this especially in the prophets. But if God is always entering into human suffering why do we need the cross? Why then speak of an act of atonement at all rather than merely of God's continuing activity of salvation? Is the cross merely a high point in God's ongoing activity? To claim that is to lose the cross as the center of the Christian faith. Fiddes admits as much: "It is one thing to find critical moments in the ongoing process of salvation, and quite another to claim that the process somehow depends upon one of those moments" (p. 25). Fiddes wants to view the cross of Jesus as the "focal point" of the whole picture, "without which the composition would fall apart" (that sounds "illustrative" to me) while holding that view together with "the equally important belief that salvation is an ever-present experience" (p. 26). While Fiddes would reject a view of atonement that sees the cross as in any way appeasing God's righteous wrath or satisfying God's broken honor through an act of propitiation, he wants to retain the idea that in the experience of the cross there was a change in God.

> If we are to speak at all seriously about suffering in God, then this must involve change of some kind, for suffering is always a movement from one state of being to another. If, then, there is some change in God's experience of the world from one moment of human response to another, we begin to see how one particular moment could be more intense and critical than others. (p. 28)

I think Fiddes is in precarious territory when he uses words such as intense, raising the issue of whether then the cross was God's intention or whether by its intensity (or some other quality of the experience) it became salvific. Of course the New Testament itself is not entirely free from the language of adoptionism, but I think here Fiddes, for all his care to protect divine sovereignty and initiative, shows his hand as holding a more subjective theory of the atonement.

For Fiddes the restoring of broken relationships is best understood by analogy to the process of healing, rather than by analogy with a legal transaction.

> Using traditional terms this might be called 'subjective,' but it will work hard at understanding the 'objective focus' of God's activity, both in past and present events. This means, I believe, understanding the cross of Jesus as an event which has a unique degree of power to evoke and create human response to the forgiving love of God. (p. 29)

Is this "unique power" more to evoke than to create is the question? And I think that for Fiddes it is. I think having committed himself to the language of relationship he is forced into a more subjective emphasis on the always troublesome question of the "how" of sanctification. We will see this subjective turn again when we look at his treatment of Abelard. For even when Fiddes is attempting to demonstrate the "objective, creative power of the cross of Jesus" in a variety of ways he invariably uses subjective ideas:

> From an existential viewpoint we can think of the power of a disclosure of something new in human experience, prompting repetition of it. From the viewpoint of narrative theory we can begin to appreciate the power of a story to create new experience within the hearer. From a viewpoint of social dynamics and the power of groups, we can begin to see the effect of a community which has lived through the ages under the cross and which links us now with the earliest disciples. With the help of psychological theory we can glimpse the power of an event outside ourselves to break open a self-enclosed ego. (p. 29)

It becomes clear that for Fiddes, the cross of Christ is primarily an "enabling event," to use one of his own phrases. He concludes Part I with an argument for taking the "facts of history" seriously despite the problems in doing so. The dynamics of loving relationship that so inform his view of atonement are evidenced in the life of Jesus and in his obedient sonship to God:

> The testimony of history is that the experience of sonship was basic to the work and hopes of Jesus. If we let this shape our faith, we must understand atonement as the bringing of many human sons and daughters into the fellowship of God's own life. This confirms once again that the atonement is something that can happen here and now. The creating of children of God can be no mere conferring of a label and a status through an arrangement made in the past, but the opening of the human self to God in trust. (p. 58)

In Part II Fiddes demonstrates that the various prevailing images for atonement, while highlighting various necessary facets about it, create problems of their own which obscure the truth of the atonement. He begins with sacrifice and traces its various meanings through the testaments. He rejects that Christ's death was in any way a propitiation. He is more sympathetic to ideas of expiation, but even so the scripture never tells us how such a sacrifice is an act of power. He concludes that we will need to look elsewhere, to other images for why "the death of Jesus should be an event of unique power, purifying human lives here and now" (p. 82).

He moves on to the juridical images noting the difficulties we have previously seen: the moral objections, the notions of a necessity laid somehow on God, and the tendency of these views to speak of transactions far removed from human life. As he looks at the legal metaphors, once again he moves toward a more subjective interpretation,

saying that Jesus the obedient Son comes under judgment
in the human law court and also before God his Father not
to endure "a penalty instead of us, but to create a penitence
in us" (p. 110).

Fiddes then turns to the image of a decisive victory,
first noting the various tyrants that the victory is over: sin,
law, death, Satan as the embodiment of evil, and the principalities and powers. Christ is the one who decisively con-
quers all the hostile powers that trap and spoil human life,
but only through the cost of great suffering. It is a demonstration of the power of weakness and an enabling event for
those who follow, making them victors over the powers that
would subject them. Here Fiddes turns to some of the modern theological reflections on sin as idolatry, understood as
the worship of that which is not God. "Jesus smashes the
idols through his unfaltering obedience and trust in him" (p.
135). He thereby creates a new possibility which lies open
for those who come after (through the power of revelation,
as in the existential theology of John Macquarrie). Likewise the new community that he has created (the community of the crucified in Macquarrie's phrase) repeats his victory in their life together on behalf of the world. But it is the
act of love that all these images need to fill them out and
Fiddes turns next to that.

He wants to defend Abelard from the charge that he
is an exemplarist reductionist who merely viewed the
atonement as a beautiful moral example that we should
now emulate. Fiddes is not blind to the problems in Abelard
and spends not a little time examining them, but he believes
that the power of redemptive love that Abelard emphasized
in his interpretation is a necessary part of an adequate doctrine of the atonement. For Abelard, when God revealed
himself in the life of Jesus and reconciled us to himself by
his death, he did not have to satisfy any prior conditions
such as the demand of Satan or his own justice. "Rather he
was simply satisfying his own nature in love. The very es-

sence of God is love, and so the original act of creation and the new act of redemption were only 'necessary' in the sense that they fulfilled his own being" (p. 143). Since for Abelard humanity needs to be reconciled to God and God doesn't need to be reconciled to anyone, love is both the means and the motive for atonement.

Such love is more than just an object lesson, but carries within it the power to change lives. Abelard believes the revelation of God's love to have a redemptive impact on its own. As the love is revealed it is poured out. Drawing on insights from Reinhold Niebuhr's exposition of Pauline ideas of wisdom and power and on ideas from modern psychology, especially the Freudian interpretation of atonement of R. S. Lee, Fiddes puts forth the view that the witness of the cross can make us recognize our limits, and shatter the self-centeredness of the ego, bringing us to contrition and faith.

It is from Abelard that Fiddes has derived the analogy of healing. Our estrangement from God is not some impersonal debt to be paid off, but rather a broken relationship that needs to be healed. Fiddes notes the individualism of this view as a problem. Where is the more corporate understanding to be found that can round out this view? Fiddes looks to the Eastern Church's tradition of *theosis* or deification to show the link between Christ's new creation and ours. The power of the Holy Spirit to effect the renewal of divine nature in us is also present in the thought of Athanasius. Fiddes sees in him another explanation for the link between the new creation in Christ and us:

> "By grace [God] becomes the Father of those whose Maker he already is; he becomes this when created men receive, as the Apostle says, the Spirit of His Son crying, 'Abba Father' in their hearts. It is these who, having received the Word, have gained power from him to become God's children. Being creatures by nature, they would never have become sons if they had not

> received the Spirit from Him who is the true son
> by nature" (*Contra Arianos*, quoted in Fiddes,
> p. 153).

"The Holy Spirit of God, on this view, applies to us the renewal of the divine image in Christ's nature" (p. 153). Abelard did not associate the love of the Holy Spirit with the cross of Christ, so the pouring out of the Spirit became dissociated from atonement. Fiddes thinks that the Spirit does not merely 'apply' the past work of atonement, but is present here and now to transform our personalities (Alan P. F. Sell suggests that many theologians show a weakness on the role of the Holy Spirit in the appropriation of atonement. "Indeed, with this in mind, I should prefer to ask 'How is the atonement brought home to us?' rather than 'How is the atonement appropriated [as if we do it ourselves]?'" (personal correspondence).

In Part III Fiddes refers to "experiences," which include the cost of forgiveness, political engagement, and the problems of suffering. I think Fiddes addresses these more existential issues so that his method reflects the impetus of his theology as one that deals with the issues of contemporary life.

Having committed himself to the language of relationships as his prevailing metaphor Fiddes understands the experience of forgiveness as central to atonement. In looking at forgiveness Fiddes notes that for true reconciliation to take place there must be a movement from both sides, the forgiven as well as the forgiver.

> Forgiveness is a costly and difficult matter both
> for the one who offers it and the one who re-
> ceives it, because true forgiveness aims for rec-
> onciliation, and this means the removal of bar-
> riers to relationship. Early on I referred to
> forgiveness as a shattering experience and
> stressed that when atonement is understood as
> an act of divine forgiveness, it must be an event

> that happens here and now. Forgiveness is no
> mere legal pardon, as became clear in our analy-
> sis of the New Testament concept of 'justifica-
> tion'; it is not an impersonal notice of acquittal
> which could be issued long ago and left lying
> around for us to pick up in due time, but a heal-
> ing of relationship that must involve us now as
> the ones who are estranged. (pp. 172-173)

Fiddes sees a two-fold dynamic in forgiveness, one
that corresponds to the life and death of Jesus. He calls it
the journey of forgiveness to show that it is a process. The
first part is a journey of discovery in which the sleeping
wrong is awakened and drawn out. The second part is the
journey of endurance in which one passively bears the consequences of having brought out the sleeping wrong. This
is just what God in Christ did for sinful humanity in the
cross, and in doing so was changed in some way:

> Through the twofold journey of forgiveness,
> through the stages of awakening, awareness and
> absorbing hostility, the forgiver is learning how
> best to win the offender to himself. The fruit of
> this agonising journey is the ability to draw a
> hostile and stubborn heart into forgiving love.
> Though talk of God's 'learning' can only be a
> metaphorical way of speaking of his taking new
> human experience into himself, yet there is
> surely a hint that God's Spirit is able to wrestle
> with human spirits today and draw them into
> reconciliation because he has made the journey
> of discovery in the cross. (p. 178)

It is this same dynamic of action and submission
that Fiddes brings to inform the discussion of political engagement. Noting the themes of Liberation theologies, he
sees Christ's death as the outcome of his conflict with the
religious and political powers of his time, so the cross can
be seen as the reaction of human sin to divine love. This
more historical view contrasts with those theories of atonement that present God as planning the cross to satisfy his
anger against human sin.

> . . . if the Father is envisaged as requiring the
> death of Christ as a reparation for his offended
> justice, the cross will only legitimise other pat-
> terns of oppression in our world. If the Father is
> an oppressor, for whatever apparently good rea-
> sons, this sets up a pattern in which oppression
> can always be justified as being for the ultimate
> benefit of society. If God is not only the su-
> preme victim but also the supreme executioner,
> he will become the patron of human execution-
> ers and torturers. (p. 192)

Rather, the cross presents us with a pattern of political engagement modeled after the action/submission of Jesus, which is the dynamic of the journey of forgiveness and
the way of divine love.

Fiddes concludes the book with an exploration of
theodicy in the light of the atonement theory he has presented. The only justification of God is the assertion that
God is both present in the suffering and protests against it.
That provides us with a pattern to deal with suffering in our
lives, to accept suffering, but not in mere resignation. Rather to face up to the suffering that comes our way and make
it our own. The cross reminds us that there was a moment
in the story when meaning was lost and Jesus cried out in
forsakenness, but beyond was the resurrection. God gives
the cross meaning, as he reveals himself to have been
present there, making his story available so that all other
human stories can acquire meaning.

This is a sophisticated attempt to formulate a theory
of atonement in the light of the various problems associated
with traditional theories and in a manner which addresses
many modern concerns. A student could do worse than to
work through this book to become acquainted with the issues in atonement. Fiddes' use of literary examples to illustrate the theory is very effective. I think he makes a good
case for the strengths of the Abelardian tradition against its
detractors and offers a well thought-out modern atonement

theory that is in that tradition. Clearly divine love and the language of relationships must figure in any adequate theory.

At the same time Fiddes is open to the charge that his is just a more sophisticated exemplarist theory where the 'how' of sanctification is revelation, illustration, and example. The divine sovereignty and initiative are also at risk in this theory, where the cross somehow "happens" to God, and he must come to terms with it as a new experience that "changes" him. The difficulty of explaining the connection between past event with present salvation remains, and will offer challenges for theologians yet unborn. Faith assures us that there is a connection though it eludes precise articulation.

VI

HOW THEN SHALL WE SPEAK OF THE ATONEMENT?

The Apostle Paul wrote to the Christians in Rome ". . . God shows his love for us in that while we were yet sinners Christ died for us." The death of Christ was understood by the earliest church, not least by Paul himself, as a divine act of reconciliation between God and humanity. Which is to say that Christ's death on the cross was understood from the beginning as an atoning death. Nevertheless, there has never been an official doctrine of the atonement, no ecumenically agreed upon articulation approved by a council of the church as there is, for example, for the doctrine of the Trinity. This is not to imply that the atonement is not a central affirmation of the Christian faith. English words such as "crux" and "crucial," which are rooted in the Latin for cross (crux), should remind us of the place that Christ's cross held for earlier generations of Christians. The Christian "idea" (Fiddes) or "understanding" (Dillistone) of atonement has been given shape through the centuries by Christian theologians attempting to redescribe in conceptual terms the atoning or reconciling activity of God in Christ as depicted in the biblical accounts of the life, death and resurrection of Jesus Christ.

These "theories" of atonement have tended to focus on the mechanism by which atonement is accomplished, the "how" of God's saving act in Christ. Twentieth century theology has been heir to two main strands of atonement theories. A more conservative strand has retained the language of the biblical affirmations and cast its theories in the thought-world of an earlier orthodoxy, heedless of the hermeneutical gap that atonement faces in engaging a contemporary audience. Such theories seem overly objective, transactional, and mechanical in their understanding of what God does in the atonement. Liberal theology, on the other hand, has tended to reduce the atonement to an object lesson, an illustration of the eternal mercy of God and lost the objectivity of the atonement and therefore its centrality for Christian faith. These two tendencies, drawn starkly here as ideal types, correspond roughly to the two main traditions in Western atonement theology: the more objective "satisfaction" theories using legal language typified by Anselm, and the more subjective moral theories typified by Abelard. Today's successors to these two main types have had little opportunity to be in conversation with one another, and the great church is poorer for this.

In the past decade, however, there has been a flurry of renewed interest in the atonement in British theology, marked by the nearly simultaneous appearance in 1988-1989 of two significant books on the subject: *The Actuality of the Atonement: A Study of Metaphor, Rationality and the Christian Tradition* by Colin E. Gunton and *Past Event and Present Salvation: The Christian Idea of Atonement* by Paul S. Fiddes. That these books represent quite different approaches and traditions in calling for a new look at atonement can only be for the good. A third important book taking up the challenge appeared in 1991, *The Atonement and Incarnation: An Essay in Universalism and Particularity* by Vernon White. During my study I have read these newer offerings as well as works about atonement in biblical studies such as *The Atonement: A Study of the Origins of the Doctrine in the New Testament* by Martin Hengel (1981) and *The Cry of Jesus on the Cross: A Biblical and Theological Study* by Gérard Rossé (1987). I have also returned to the works of earlier writers, particularly P. T. Forsyth's *The*

Work of Christ, and *The Person and Place of Jesus Christ.*

Already in the above description of two traditions in atonement theology I employed terms such as "objective," "subjective," "satisfaction," and "moral" to describe different theories. The vocabulary of atonement needs careful scrutiny if we are to find adequate ways to think about and articulate the meaning of atonement. In addition, I have noticed in my reading that several salient issues have appeared again and again among the various writers. These critical issues provide a framework in which to think carefully about the atonement, and offer a set of guidelines for the important task of articulating an adequate theory. They are perennial issues that reappear whenever an attempt is made to redescribe in conceptual language the truths of the biblical narrative. I will explore these issues and the vocabulary in which they are expressed.

The first of these perennial issues is the pair of opposite tendencies called Objective/ Subjective which I have already employed to describe the Anselmian and Abelardian traditions. By "objective" we mean those theories that stress the divine initiative and activity in atonement, and by "subjective" we mean those theories that stress the human response in atonement. While it is true that every articulation of the atonement that takes the biblical narrative seriously will have both objective and subjective elements, most theologies of the atonement will stress one or the other of these tendencies. What is decisive for any adequate theory is that it is objective enough to clearly affirm that God has definitively acted to deal with evil and sin, and at the same time contains subjective elements that address the manner of the human appropriation of the effects of that salvation. Thus both "justification," what God does for us, and "sanctification," the way we live in response to that divine act of salvation, must be kept in view.

A related pair of opposites is Constitutive/

Illustrative. Does a particular theory of the atonement hold that the saving work of Christ on the cross is "constitutive" for salvation, the divine act itself accomplishing something for us, or is the cross of Christ merely "illustrative," demonstrating to us the divine love or mercy that was always there for us? Theories that are constitutive can have significant features of the more illustrative theories present in them, so that, for example, the cross reveals and demonstrates the salvation that God intends for us. For them, however, it is the event of the cross itself that effects salvation whereas for purely illustrative theories it does not. A related word to illustrative is exemplarist, which refers to an exemplar or model. In an exemplarist Christology Jesus is seen primarily as a model for us to follow, and so in this view the cross then is often construed as the apotheosis of human sacrifice which we then ought to emulate in our conduct. Theories in this tradition are also called moral theories.

The next set of issues is not a pair of opposites, but rather two typical ways of referring to the work of Christ in salvation: was his death a substitution or representation? Is it that Christ in his humanity "represents" us before God and thereby does something decisive for our salvation, or need we say more, that Christ's death is a "substitution," a taking of our place and thereby doing for us what we could not do for ourselves? The distinction is nuanced but frequently signals a real difference. In some theologies representation and substitution are used interchangeably, but other modern theologians prefer representation as a way to avoid the negative connotations that have accrued around the more mechanical theories of substitution. From our study of the biblical material (i.e., Hengel and Rossé) it seems clear that "substitution" was an important way of interpreting Jesus' death from the earliest days of the Christian community (in Pre-Markan kerygma and in Paul, for example) and may well have been a feature of Jesus' self-understanding by which he taught the disciples how to understand his death (as, for example, at the Last Supper). For this reason it seems that an adequate articulation of atonement will use the language of substitution, albeit with some care.

One highly imaginative attempt to articulate how Christ represents humanity before God was the nineteenth century Scottish theologian J. McLeod Campbell's use of the term confession. McLeod Campbell was attempting to break away from the rigid transactional theories of atonement typical of the Scottish Calvinism of his day (and for his pains was deposed as a minister of the Church of Scotland for denying the doctrine of limited atonement). He proposed that Christ's work was a two-fold exhibition, showing God's love to humankind and of humankind's penitence before God. In his view Christ offers a perfect penitence on our behalf, making confession before God in our name (*The Nature of the Atonement and its Relation to Remission of Sins and Eternal Life*, 1878). The question is raised of this view "how can Christ confess those sins he did not share?" We see a related idea in P. T. Forsyth who has a chapter in *The Work of Christ* called "The Great Confessional," in which it is not sin that Christ confesses, but rather "God's holiness in reacting mortally against human sin, in cursing human sin, in judging it to its very death" (*Work of Christ*, p. 150). Forsyth's approach is much the stronger, but in both cases they seem to be moving well out of the region supported by the biblical evidence into speculation. Clearly Christ in his humanity represents all of humanity before God, but more needs to be said about how atonement takes place. Representation, therefore, will be a necessary part of any adequate atonement theory, not as a replacement for "substitution" but as a related concept that enriches our understanding of atonement.

The next pair of words refers to two ways of interpreting Jesus' death as a sacrifice. Was his death an expiation or propitiation? We will turn in a moment to the complicated issues around sacrifice, but for now the decisive

question around these terms is this: is the atonement per-
formed towards us or towards God? Both "expiation" and
"propitiation" are terms used of sacrifice, but expiation implies a sacrificial taking away of some sin or offence (i.e.,
Christ died for our sins), whereas propitiation implies assuaging the anger or injured honor or holiness of God. An
expiation changes us, taking away our sin, whereas a propitiation changes God, satisfying whatever needed to be satisfied. These are not mutually exclusive, obviously, but again
we see how different theories will stress one or the other.
For example, in Abelard's theory, nothing is offered to God,
the atonement is a demonstration of God's eternal love,
whereas in Anselm's theory the atonement is an offering to
God, reconciling sinful humanity to God. The former risks,
among other things, falling into subjectivism and failing to
take God's anger, honor, or justice seriously enough. The
latter is criticized chiefly for turning the anger, honor or
justice of God into a third thing beyond the Father and the
Son, a necessity to which God is somehow obligated. A further criticism of propitiation language is that it promotes
views of atonement that have elements of punishment in
them, thereby making its view of God morally objectiona-
ble. There is always a danger when the justice or the anger
of God is separated from God's love.

It is helpful to keep in mind that the language used
to describe God's atoning work in Jesus Christ is metaphor-
ical, borrowing its vocabulary and ways of thinking from
other areas of life, principally the temple, the battlefield,
and the law court. Since the metaphors associated with
these areas are either dead, dying or have become decisively altered in meaning, they need to be examined carefully
(though dead metaphors may be essential for understanding
atonement, as Colin Gunton has argued about the language
of sacrifice. It is also true that historical events may revivi-
fy a long dead metaphor; the term "Balkanization" comes
to mind).

In fact, the entire enterprise of framing an atonement theory can be seen as a direct result of the decaying of the prevailing metaphors. The Christian writers of the New Testament and the early post-apostolic period were content to repeat the key words, "sacrifice," "propitiation," "redemption," without offering a theory of how they operated. It was quite sufficient that they stood for the truth of the Christian experience of the cross of Jesus Christ. It is only as that experience became historically less proximate and the metaphors decayed according to some unknown law of linguistic half-life, that attempts were made to explore the meaning of the metaphors more closely by means of a conceptual theory.

It is time now to turn briefly to the three most significant metaphors for atonement in the Bible, the language of sacrifice, the law court, and the battlefield. Without going into a lengthy discussion of the nature of metaphor, let us define metaphor as the use of the language of one area of life to describe another area. We need to remember also that the various metaphors interact with and impact one another, so that the discrete picture I now draw is somewhat artificial.

The first and foremost metaphor for atonement is "Christ the sacrifice." By the time of the New Testament the idea of sacrifice had already undergone a complex shift in meaning. The original and literal meaning of sacrifice is the ritual slaughter of some living being for religious or social purposes. As Frances Young has pointed out, behind this idea of sacrifice was the primitive notion of feeding the gods, typical of Graeco-Roman culture. If the gods were fed, they were happy and if not, they were displeased; so that propitiation is early on associated with sacrifice. Blood was thought to contain the life of an animal in some concentrated manner and blood sacrifice therefore was assumed to have great efficacy. But animal sacrifice was by no means the only kind, and a wide variety of sacrificial

practices were common to the ancient world. Although Israel shared these ideas and practices with its neighbors, the
theological context of the faith of Israel transformed them.
The Old Testament practices, though widely divergent, typically used animals or some substitute like grain, and were
offered for a variety of purposes such as thanksgiving, expi-
ating sin, binding a covenant, remembering God's saving
activity or merely to express communion with God. This
literal use stands behind some of the metaphors that refer to
Christ's death as a sacrifice, but the literal use by no means
encompasses the rich variety of sacrificial language. We
need to note that the idea of sacrifice was already used metaphorically long before the time of Jesus, as we can see in
such Old Testament texts as this: "The sacrifice acceptable
to God is a broken spirit; a broken and contrite heart, O
God, thou will not despise" (Isaiah 51:17). Here sacrifice is
spiritualized, taken from the context of the temple to the
context of personal piety.

The metaphor for sacrifice undergoes some even
more remarkable changes when used about the death of
Christ. First, his sacrifice is "once and for all" making all
other sacrifices obsolete (thereby ensuring the eventual
death of the metaphor itself, since its original context is no
longer available as a referent). Secondly, since Christ's sacrifice is a free and voluntary act, he acts as priest as well as
victim (we see this in *Hebrews*), demonstrating a very altered use of the idea of sacrifice. That Christ is priest as
well as victim changes the whole meaning of sacrifice and
remains important if we are to avoid an atonement theory
that pictures God as vengeful and Christ as a passive victim. The death of Christ, now understood with this new
idea of sacrifice, is not a punitive substitution but a priestly
self-offering, a sacrifice only understood in a new highly altered way.

In addition, this newly constructed sacrificial language makes its way into the discourse of the early church

in a wide variety of contexts relating to their life and faith. As Frances Young has noted, for the early Christian community, the language of sacrifice was used not only of the death of Christ, but of large areas of Christian worship and practice, which helped them to avoid falling into the trap of divorcing atonement theory from faith and response (*Sacrifice and the Death of Christ*, p. 95).

Sacrificial language, despite the loss of its original referent and its metamorphous due to the pouring into it of Christian content, remains the primary metaphor for atonement. As Colin Gunton has said, about the metaphor of sacrifice:

> Does not its orientation to life, grace, and self-giving, to the concentrated love of God poured out for the creature, take us as far as any human language can into the very heart of God? What, then, is potentially an abused and overused metaphor can also become the most living and expressive of all, the heart of the doctrine as an expression of the unfathomable power and grace of God. (*Actuality of Atonement*, p. 141)

Any adequate atonement theory must use the language of sacrifice.

The second cluster of metaphors that have shaped the way we talk about atonement comes from the language of the law court. "Justification," "satisfaction," and "penalty," for example, are legal terms. Several of the Latin Fathers were jurists and there began a tradition in the Western church to conceive of the relationship of God to humankind in the language of legal obligation. It was St. Anselm who gave this approach it first extensive systematic treatment, using the language of satisfaction. Previous theories had tended to employ the term "ransom" (from Mark 10:45) as the act that God had accomplished in atonement. In this view because of the Fall the devil had obtained sovereignty over human souls, and freedom from this dominion was ac-

complished by means of a payment in the blood of Christ.
Anselm saw the dualism that this view implied and rejected
it. Instead, Anselm employed the term "penal satisfaction,"
a metaphor drawn from law, to take seriously the requirements of divine justice and the reality of human sin. The
Son freely offers to the Father his life as compensation for
the failure of the human creation. His death outweighs in
value all the sins of humankind, so much so that the effect
reaches to those who live in another place and time. His
view is often criticized as being too transactional and there
is that sense about it, but it also employs the personal language of the Trinity and has the strength of a clear objectivity that takes both the requirements of God's justice and the
perniciousness of human sin seriously. Legal language, despite the drawback of often seeming mechanical or transactional, is a necessary means of speaking about the justice of
God and will continue to be indispensable to an adequate
atonement theory. As Forsyth put it in his critique of theological liberalism, "The chief defect of the great revolution
which began with Schleiermacher and ended in Ritschl has
been that it allowed no place to that side [ie. the juridical]
of Christ's work" (*The Work of Christ*, p. 228).

   The third set of metaphors which we need to look at
comes from the battlefield and provides us with the image
of "Christ the victor." Gustaf Aulen's thesis about a "classic
theory" has been for the most part discredited, but *Christus
Victor* did in its time spur interest in atonement studies and
offered to liberal theology a theory of atonement with the
objectivity it had been lacking. Despite Aulen's exaggerat-
ed claims for the image of victor, there is a cluster of images in the New Testament that uses the language of victory
to describe the atonement. Christ's death is a victory over
the demonic powers, the principalities and powers of this
age that control the world. To call the cross a victory is a
powerful reversal of the usual meaning of the word. Once
again we see a shift in the meaning of a word, in this in-
stance "victory," as the content of the Christ event is

poured into it. To claim such a thing for the cross is to call into question the old power arrangements of the world, so that the cross is both metaphorically and actually a victory over them. A military victory, the original meaning, is a course of action leading to a successful result. The victory of the cross shows the course of action of Jesus going to the cross, and thereby offers a new paradigm for what constitutes victory. This image tells us what it means to talk of a God who saves, and something of the way that God goes about it. The image of Christ the victor also points beyond itself, functioning eschatologically, so that the past victory is a promised future victory as well. This addresses the "already but not yet" character of the Christian promise.

The final kind of language I wish to draw to our attention is the language of relationships. As we have seen one of the typical problems of many atonement theories is their tendency toward a mechanical view of the divine activity. God, however, is a person, and the language of personal activity seems both closer to modern sensibilities and to the biblical narrative than the various transactions that have been typical of much earlier atonement theology. An adequate articulation of atonement will need to see the act of atonement within the doctrine of the Trinity and its emphasis on the inter-dependence of the divine persons. Jesus' experience of being abandoned by God, in which he endures the condition of the sinner before God, can be viewed as arising from a Trinitarian act in history, an act for which God intentionally sent him and which in obedience Jesus accepted. The atonement is therefore a Trinitarian act of mutual consent between the Father and the Son in the Holy Spirit. This way of seeing it rightly balances so called "objective" and "subjective" elements in a way that is congruent with the biblical narrative. The language of interpersonal relationships is crucial to an adequate atonement theory. It is, after all, the divine love and mercy that are the impetus for the Christ event, and "love" and "mercy" are words of interpersonal relationship.

As I have indicated above, another concern in formulating an atonement theory is that it remains faithful to the biblical narratives. If we recognize that doctrines are conceptual redescriptions of the biblical narratives, it will be important for such a redescription to be faithful to the narrative itself. Such theories do not capture and convey the truth of the narratives better than the narratives themselves. In a sense the meaning of the narratives is irreducible and must be taken on its own terms. That is to say, that however successful an atonement theory may be, it is only through interaction with the biblical account of the life, death and resurrection of Jesus that we can understand the truth of the Christian idea of atonement. A theory can help to shed light on the meaning of the narrative by use of new metaphors to help bridge the hermeneutical gap between the biblical world and our own (or Anselm's or Calvin's for that matter), but such theories draw their life from and do not replace the biblical accounts. Therefore, the closest possible attention to the narratives must be paid.

At the other end of the equation is the context in which the audience of an atonement theory find themselves and how they understand their context. The way the human predicament is understood will have an important influence on the way one understands the saving act of God. What is it from which God saves us? An age that saw itself as under the dominion of hostile demonic powers would be drawn to the image of Christ as the cosmic victor. An age that worried about social chaos would be drawn to the image of Christ the upholder of the divine justice. An age that viewed social relationships between Lord and vassal in terms of honor would be drawn to the image of Christ as the one who gives satisfaction to the offended honor of God. And an age that was preoccupied with personal sin would be drawn to the image of Christ as the one who justifies the sinner. The hermeneutical problem for the Christian communicator today is that the traditional theories of atonement offer a solution for problems that modern people do not see as problems.

The Christian idea of sin reflects a realistic assessment that the life which God intended for us is perennially and profoundly distorted. But is this a characteristic way for people today, even Christians, to view the human predicament? Do we really need to be saved from sin? More typically the human predicament is viewed as a failure to live up to human potential, or it is viewed as alienation from ourselves and others. For others there is a growing sense of human estrangement from the natural world in what is sometimes called the ecological crisis. The quest for security, for economic advancement, is the secular equivalent of salvation for many today. To such a world view, what can the proclamation mean that God in Christ has accomplished an atonement for us ?

The two typical traditions we have seen each in its own way have undermined the power of the idea of atonement. Objective theories couched in the language of legal obligation have made the idea of atonement sound too transactional, far removed from human life and Christian faith. The subjective moral views have lost the objective sense that God has acted decisively in the cross, and they have so individually construed their theory that any corporate meaning is lost.

An adequate atonement theory that will speak to the human predicament today will need to address the need for atonement at the corporate and even the cosmic level, so that it is not merely individuals as individuals that are in need of saving, but rather all of humanity and all of creation that is in need of reconciling. Such a theory will have to take both human evil and divine justice with profound seriousness. It will use the language of personal relationships, the language of love and forgiveness and mercy. It will keep its eye firmly fixed on the biblical narrative, on the life, teaching, death, and resurrection of Jesus Christ. It will insist on the objectivity of the divine act, as well as on the necessity of responding in the faith that that act has now made possible. It will look to the future in hope and promise for the final disclosure of the atonement that has already taken place and will invite and inspire men and women to live now in its light. These are my suggestions on how we might speak of atonement today, knowing as I do that no conceptualization will capture its truth for all time. At the same time I am convinced that the continuing witness of the biblical narratives to the work of Christ and the abiding inspiration of the Holy Spirit will ensure that the truth contained in the idea of atonement will abide.

VII

THE LORD WILL PROVIDE

A Sermon On Genesis 22

Abraham is the one who received the promise from God. God's promise is that Abraham will have his own land and have many descendants, and through his descendants all the peoples of the world will be blessed. This is not only a big promise, but also an astonishing one, given that Abraham is a landless nomad and a childless old man, and his wife Sarah is barren.

Nevertheless, Abraham believes God's word of promise and the promise is kept. Sarah becomes pregnant and bears a son, whom they name Isaac, which means laughter, for Sarah laughs when God tells her she will have a son. Young Isaac is now the bearer of the promise, but in today's story the promise is threatened.

As with many biblical stories, we know more than the characters do. We know that God is testing Abraham, but Abraham doesn't know this. God commands him to take his son, his only son whom he loves, to the land of Moriah to sacrifice him. The form of the command from God echoes the original promise to Abraham. So the God who made the promise seems to be putting the promise in jeopardy. Abraham hears God's command. He has already lost his first born son, Ishmael, whom he sent away into the desert with his mother Hagar, so the loss of Isaac will be the end of Abraham's family, as well as the end of the promise.

Israel would have heard this story as their own story, for in their story the promise is always threatened. And the threat to the promise is the threat to their continued existence. Yet Israel would also have heard it as the story of how, though the promise is always in jeopardy, somehow God "sees" that the promise is kept, that the story continues.

So Abraham does as God has commanded him. He prepares for the sacrifice, takes Isaac and heads out to the land of Moriah on a three day's journey. After three days Abraham looks up and sees the place from far away. Father and son climb the hill and Isaac asks Abraham, "Where is the lamb for a burnt offering?" Abraham answers "God himself will provide the lamb for a burnt offering, my son."

God will provide. The word providence itself derives from this passage, and also from verse 14, after God has produced a ram. Then Abraham called the place, "The Lord will provide" or "The Lord has seen:" *Jehova Jireh.*

And God does provide. He produces a ram. Abraham passes the test. He is prepared to sacrifice his son, and with him Abraham's own prospects as the carrier of the promise. But God doesn't require the sacrifice of Isaac.

It is a disturbing story. It raises any number of troubling questions, and from the beginning interpreters have tried to figure out its implications, from the ancient rabbis to Søren Kierkegaard's *Fear and Trembling.* In our own time a psycholoanalyst has suggested that the story is a story of child abuse, and has burdened our religious heritage with a climate in which abuse is tolerated (see Alice Miller, *The Untouched Key: Tracing Childhood Trauma in Creativity and Destructiveness.* New York: Doubleday, 1990, p.

139). A tradition can be misused, of course, but let us leave the psychological and philosophical interpretations aside today and look at this story within the larger biblical story of the promise.

In its own context within Genesis this episode is the climax of the larger story of the promise. It is a story about human faith, but above all, about divine providence, about the way God keeps his promise from generation to generation in the lives of these ordinary people.

Notice how few details we are told about God. In this story there is no burning bush, no ladder to heaven, just the simple command of God. Does Abraham see God? Does the command come in a dream, in a voice, in a cloud? We don't know. Although God is the chief actor in the drama of promise and fulfillment, he remains in the background, speaking from mystery, his intentions not fully known.

In comparing this story with the Odyssey of Homer, literary critic Eric Auerbach notices that, unlike the Greek god Zeus, who is comprehensible in his presence, the God of the Bible is not; "it is always 'something of him' that appears, he always extends into depths." The Greek narratives with their gods take place in the foreground, while the biblical narrative with its God remains mysterious and is 'fraught with background.' Here in Genesis we are not told everything as Homer would tell us, we are told only what we need to know. Homer's poem is almost photographic in its detail, but here we have few details. We don't know what Abraham was thinking, what Isaac looked like, what kind of day it was. We are not told of inner states of mind. The narrative is spare. And it is not Abraham's character, courage or pride that is decisive for the story, but his previous history, as the one to whom God has made the promise (Eric Auerbach, *Mimesis*, p. 12).

The story keeps us off balance. Its outcome is not predictable. And the spareness of the biblical narrative means we have to look for clues to discern what is going on. One of the clues here is the idea of "seeing." Throughout the Genesis story there is the motif of seeing, the human characters seeing, and God seeing. For example when Hagar is told by an angel of the Lord that she will give birth to Ishmael. She says, "Have I really seen God and remained alive after seeing him?"

The human characters see, but only now and then, bit by bit. Seeing is never complete. They see, to use Paul's phrase "through a glass darkly." The characters see only part of the way. But seeing seems to be essential for faith. The characters need to see, at least in part, what God is up to. They need to see how the promise is fulfilled. They won't see completely, they must act in faith, and perhaps it is faith that lets them see as much as they do.

So Abraham travels for three days and looks up and sees the place for the sacrifice. And when he is about to sacrifice Isaac he looks up and sees the ram. Was the ram already there? Had God prepared for the sacrifice in advance? Could Abraham only see the ram when he trusted the Lord and met the test? We don't know.

In any case "God says, 'Do not lay your hand on the boy or do anything to him; for now I know that you fear God, since you have not withheld your son, your only son from me.' And Abraham looked up and saw a ram, caught in a thicket by the horns. Abraham went and took the ram, and offered it up as a burnt offering instead of his son. So Abraham called that place 'The Lord will provide.'" The Hebrew means "The Lord will see."

So God also sees! But this Hebrew verb "to see" is a "warm verb," so God is not merely a passive seer, but an active **doer** in response to what he sees. Providence means not just that the Lord sees, but that he "sees to it." In the Latin, "to see:" *Pro video*. God will see to it!

So Question 27 of *The Heidelberg Catechism*: "What does thou understand by the providence of God? Answer: The almighty and present power of God by which he still upholds and therefore rules as with his hand heaven and earth and every creature, and that leaves and grass, rain and drought, fruitful and unfruitful years, food and drink, health and sickness, riches and poverty and all other things do not come by accident but from his fatherly hand."

The Lord will provide. He both sees and "sees to it." Divine providence has often been understood as foreseeing, but that is only half of it. So Karl Barth writes:

> . . . The God who so wonderfully foresees and provides is not a mere supreme being but the God who, in this happening in which Abraham was to spare his son, acted as the Lord of the covenant of grace that Abraham was promised and given his successor Isaac, that he had then (as a prophecy of the One who was to come) to separate and bring him as an offering to God, but that he had not to die but to live as a type of the One who was to come and give life through His real death, a substitute being found for him in the form of a ram. (Karl Barth, *CD* 3.3,35)

I am convinced that the earliest Christians were prepared to interpret the death of Jesus as an atoning, sacrificial act by God because they knew this story of Abraham and Isaac. As good Jews they trusted the identity of God as the One who both sees and "sees to it," and so the crucifixion and resurrection were seen as the ultimate act of divine providence, doing for us what we could not and can not do for ourselves, saving us from sin and death.

A son climbs a holy hill with wood on his back for a sacrifice. *They recognized that story!* They knew it was a terrible story. But they were able to see in faith that God sees, and in Easter light, they saw with the clarity of 20/20 hindsight, that God did provide the sacrifice, that the promise was kept and the story continues.

BIBLIOGRAPHY

BOOKS

Athanasius. "Against the Arians," *The Nicene and Post-Nicene Fathers.*—2nd Series, vol. 4. Edinburgh: T&T Clark, 1987.

Auerbach, Eric. *Mimesis: The Representation of Reality in Western Literature.* Princeton: Princeton University Press, 1953.

Aulén, Gustaf. *Christus Victor.* New York: Macmillan, 1969.

Barth, Karl. *Church Dogmatics.* Vol. 3:3. Edinburgh: T&T Clark, 1960.

Bauckham, Richard. *God Crucified: Monotheism and Christology in the New Testament.* Grand Rapids: William B. Eerdmans, 1998.

Brown, Ramond E. *The Death of the Messiah*, 2 Volumes. New York: Doubleday, 1993.

Campbell, J. Macleod. *The Nature of the Atonement.* Grand Rapids: Eerdmans, 1996.

Fiddes, Paul S. *Past Event and Present Salvation: The Christian Idea of Atonement.* London: Darton, Longman and Todd, 1989.

Forsyth, P. T. Untitled article in *The Atonement in Modern Religious Thought.* New York: Whittaker, 1901.

_____. *The Cruciality of the Cross.* London: Independent Press, 1948.

_____. *God the Holy Father.* London: Independent Press, 1957.

_____. *The Person and Place of Jesus Christ.* London: Independent Press, 1948.

_____. *The Preaching of Jesus and the Gospel of Christ.* Blackwood, South Australia: New Creation Publications, 1987.

Forsyth, cont'd. *The Work of Christ*. London: Hodder and Stoughton, 1910.

Franks, R. S. *The Work of Christ*. London: Nelson, 1962.

Grayston, K. *Dying, We Live: A New Enquiry into the Death of Christ in the New Testament*. Oxford: Oxford University Press, 1990.

Gunton, Colin E. *The Actuality of Atonement: A Study of Metaphor, Rationality and the Christian Tradition*. Edinburgh: T&T Clark, 1988.

_____. *Yesterday and Today: A Study of Continuities in Christology*. Grand Rapids: Eerdmanns, 1983.

Hart, Trevor, editor. *Justice the True and Only Mercy*. Edinburgh: T&T Clark, 1995.

Hart, Trevor A. and Daniel P. Thimell, editors. *Christ in Our Place: The Humanity of God in Christ for the Reconciliation of the World. Essays Presented to James B. Torrance*. Allison Park, PA: Pickwick Publications, 1991.

The Heidelberg Catechism with Commentary. Phildadelphia: United Church Press, 1996.

Hengel, Martin. *The Atonement: A Study of the Origins of the Doctrine in the New Testament*. London: SCM Press, 1981.

McKim, Donald, editor. "Atonement," *The Encyclopedia of the Reformed Faith*. Louisville: Westminster/John Knox, 1992.

Miller, Alice. *The Untouched Key: Tracing Childhood Trauma in Creativity and Destruction*. New York: Doubleday, 1990.

O'Collins, Gerald. *The Calvary Christ*. Oxford: Oxford University Press, 1977.

Placher, William C. *Narratives of a Vulnerable God: Christ, Theology and Scripture*. London: SPCK, 1994.

Rossé, Gérard. *The Cry of Jesus on the Cross: A Biblical and Theological Study*. New York: Paulist Press, 1987.

Sloyan, Gerard S. *The Crucifixion of Jesus: History, Myth, Faith*. Minneapolis: Fortress Press, 1995.

Sykes, Stephen W., editor. *Sacrifice and Redemption: Durham Essays in Theology*. Cambridge: Cambridge University Press, 1991.

White, Vernon. *Atonement and Incarnation: An Essay in Universalism and Particularity*. Cambridge: Cambridge University Press, 1991.

Wright, N. T. *The Climax of the Covenant: Christ and the Law in Pauline Theology*. Minneapolis: Fortress Press, 1993.

_____. *Jesus and the Victory of God*. Minneapolis: Fortress Press, 1996.

Young, Frances M. *The Use of Sacrificial Ideas in Greek Christian Writers from the New Testament to John Chrysostom*. Philadelphia: Philadephia Patristic Foundation, 1979.

ARTICLES

Boys, Mary C. "The Cross: Should a Symbol Betrayed Be Reclaimed?" *Cross Currents* (Spring 1994).

Floyd, Richard L. "The Cross and the Church: The Soteriology and Ecclesiology of P. T. Forsyth." *Andover Newton Review* 3 (1992).